Serving Up GOD

My Workplace as a Ministry

Colin MacDougall

WESTBOW
PRESS®
A DIVISION OF THOMAS NELSON
& ZONDERVAN

The Holy Bible, English Standard Version® (ESV®)
Copyright © 2001 by Crossway,
a publishing ministry of Good News Publishers.
All rights reserved.

This book is a work of non-fiction. Unless otherwise noted, the author and the publisher make no explicit guarantees as to the accuracy of the information contained in this book and in some cases, names of people and places have been altered to protect their privacy.

Front cover: From original watercolor painting by Inae Kim www.inaekim.com

WestBow Press books may be ordered through booksellers or by contacting:

WestBow Press
A Division of Thomas Nelson & Zondervan
1663 Liberty Drive
Bloomington, IN 47403
www.westbowpress.com
1 (866) 928-1240

Because of the dynamic nature of the Internet, any web addresses or links contained in this book may have changed since publication and may no longer be valid. The views expressed in this work are solely those of the author and do not necessarily reflect the views of the publisher, and the publisher hereby disclaims any responsibility for them.

Any people depicted in stock imagery provided by Thinkstock are models, and such images are being used for illustrative purposes only.
Certain stock imagery © Thinkstock.

ISBN: 978-1-5127-8801-3 (sc)
ISBN: 978-1-5127-8800-6 (hc)
ISBN: 978-1-5127-8802-0 (e)

Library of Congress Control Number: 2017907953

Print information available on the last page.

WestBow Press rev. date: 05/23/2017

ACKNOWLEDGMENTS

I would like to acknowledge and thank Mark Harris for his help and encouragement with this project. He took a great deal of time out of his busy schedule to help edit. His probing questions and observations were helpful with keeping me focused on the big picture.

I would like to thank my friends Paul and Yolanda Yeo for being willing to validate my wife, Joanne, and I as we embarked on this journey of discovering our workplace as ministry before God. The way they have chosen to view their own business as an opportunity for blessing others, has been an inspiration to us.

I would like to thank my mother, Sylvia, for teaching me not to settle for a situation in life, but to strive to improve it. I appreciate the support she has given me to become the man that I am.

I would like to thank my children for being patient with me over these years. I am a workaholic at times, and it would seem as though I put work first in many cases. They have been very understanding. Although my work is important to me, it pales in comparison to the importance of the love I feel for these three amazing humans. I am very proud of them all. I hope they will find God's purpose for their lives, and the courage to live authentically.

Finally, and most importantly, I want to thank my wife, Joanne. She has been, and will continue to be, everything to me. Without her help, I would be nothing more than a wrapper without a candy bar, a shell without a peanut, a bowl of Cornflakes without milk, a French fry without ketchup, a tic tac without a toe. I am also thankful for the encouragement that Joanne provided me to write this book. Her ability to grasp what I struggle to write and help to turn it into something understandable amazes me. Joanne and I are on a great journey together, and I am excited to see where God will take us next.

CONTENTS

INTRODUCTION

A few years ago, my wife, Joanne, and I found that we were struggling to find a purpose and a reason for our busy lives. Between raising children (which, in case you are wondering, is a real full time job) and working 40-60 hours, most weeks, at our management jobs with a local pizzeria, we found that we were missing something. Somehow, we went from saying, "I do" and being full of excitement and energy for what we could do for God, to saying, "How am I going to survive this week?" It felt like we were missing the point of serving God. Aren't Christians supposed to be involved in ministries? What about feeding the poor, teaching the Bible, and countless other recognizable ministries? We just didn't have the time. Bills needed to be paid. Mouths needed to be fed. We were in the busiest time of our lives as parents, and didn't feel that we had much else to offer. How could we serve God and keep up with life at the same time?

We began to look at where we spent most of our time. In our case, it was our workplace. We were making friends and finding that we were getting to know our staff and co-workers. There were days when we would be counsellors, days when we would be cheerleaders, days when we would be that parental voice of reason. We found we were ministering to people more and more. Simply put, our workplace was our ministry. At first, it seemed a revolutionary concept, but as time went on, we began to realize that *ministry* is exactly what we were doing. Looking back on my life, I can see now that God had been laying the groundwork for me to be able to see this. It is only now that I am really able to appreciate and understand it.

With all this in mind, a few years ago we decided that we wanted to step out on our own and open a restaurant that was ours. Right from the start we wanted to honor God with it. If this was to be a ministry, then we needed God's help and guidance.

A lot of what I have discovered, and what I am still discovering about ministry in the workplace, is found in this book.

Probably one of the greatest revelations I've had, was: Your purpose in life, simply put, is to live Christ where you are. That's it. Everything you will ever need to know in life is found in that one statement. That's the whole book right there. You can save yourself hours of reading and self-examination, put the book down and turn on the hockey game (Montreal is up 3-1, in case you are curious) or you can read on.

To live Christ. What does that really mean? For most of us, it is quite difficult to quantify. It becomes something almost abstract. For answers, we can look to Jesus and the life he lived before God and man as an example. Through his life, we see how he valued people and chose to interact with them. He called to himself a group of untrained men, and taught them to be workers for God. He spoke great words, he did amazing miracles, he showed them the way to know God. He then left them, and all of us, the Great Commission – "Go into all the world and preach the Good News."

I am convinced that *all the world* includes my workplace. So, what does it mean for me to live Christ? I look to this passage in Philippians 2 for some guidance.

"Do nothing from selfish ambition or conceit, but in humility count others more significant than yourselves. Let each of you look not only to his own interests, but also to the interests of others. Have this mind among yourselves, which is yours in Christ Jesus, who, though he was in the form of God, did not count equality with God a thing to be grasped, but emptied himself, by taking the form of a servant, being born in the likeness of men." Philippians 2:2–7

Christ took the form of a servant. Although, as King of Kings, it was his right to rule, he chose humility. He chose to empty himself. What does this humility look like? Well, it puts the interests of others ahead of our own.

As an example, there are times in my workplace when all I want to do is focus on my job and get everything done. The quicker I finish, the sooner I get to go home. I had one of those days yesterday. I was focused, I was in a groove and moving through my tasks when I got a text from a friend of mine who wanted to stop by and see me. He needed help with some things in his life. I just wanted to push through my work, but his interests needed to be ahead of mine. He popped in and we were able to share some time together. In retrospect, I was just as impacted and edified with the time together as he was. It was a simple thing, and in the scope of this great life, a few extra minutes on my day really isn't a big deal. Living life as a servant can accomplish more than we realize.

Selfish ambition and conceit are always knocking on the door. We have now been in business, on our own, for over five years. As a business owner I get asked, almost weekly, when I am going to expand or open a second location. The businessman in me thinks about this and says, "Maybe I can build my empire - one location today, major national franchise tomorrow!" It is quite tempting to consider those kinds of opportunities, but my wife and I have decided to put aside those selfish ambitions to focus solely on this one location. We can't be a part of the daily lives of those around us if we are too busy building an empire. God has shown us that being small allows for the intimacy that is needed to live Christ before our staff and customers.

It is interesting that Jesus was born in the likeness of men, but it is men who must strive to live in the likeness of Jesus.

This passage from Philippians gives a glimpse into what it is like to live life in the likeness of Jesus. I love how the step-by-step guide to making my workplace my ministry, is hidden in plain sight in these commonly quoted verses.

As you will see, I am no theologian, but I am a story teller. It is my hope, as I share bits of stories from my life and work experience, that you may find something that will encourage and, perhaps, challenge you. Some examples will be very specific. Don't hyper focus on my experience and lose sight of what may apply in your situation. Other examples are going to be a little more generic. Look at them, and use them to broaden your understanding of what God is capable of doing. Because many of the stories are quite personal, I have decided to change some of the names to protect the subjects' privacy.

Jesus used stories and parables, in addition to his life, to teach us so much. This book is a parable of sorts. The Kingdom of God in your workplace is like...well, let's find out together shall we!

Chapter 1

DRUMMER BOY MENTALITY

Work as a Gift of Worship

*A*s I begin to write this book, it is early in November. I was in one of the local grocery stores the other morning and started hearing Christmas carols. This Christmas stuff starts way too early for my liking…but I digress. One of the songs being played was *The Little Drummer Boy.* This song has always resonated with me. I can identify with that little guy who played the drum.

First, it's hard to believe for those that know me now, but I used to be a rather small fellow. I was so short that, in Grade seven, I stood on the chair of my desk and when Troy Washington stood beside me, he was still taller than I was. I have always been a little smaller in stature than most of my contemporaries.

The second reason I feel I can identify with this little guy, is because of my family's financial situation during my growing-up years. Mom was doing a great job trying to raise us three kids on her own, after she left my father. Money was tight though. We were on welfare and lived in one of the few apartment buildings in town that could be afforded by those who lived on lower incomes. We never had a lot of excess, but that was okay. Incidentally, people often ask me where I get my work ethic from. Well, in part, it is from seeing my mother strive to provide for us. She wasn't content to live on welfare. She wanted to be self-sufficient, and worked hard to do so. It took until I was in high school, but she did it. I am very proud of what she did. I guess I'm inspired too! In short, like the boy in the song, I was a boy with humble beginnings.

So, set the picture in your mind, I was a small boy with little monetary resources. I wasn't blessed with the ability to play music. In fact, it is quite the opposite. I am so out of sync with music that I have a hard time playing the radio in tune. What gifts or treasures of worship could I have to lay before the King? When I was that little kid, I am not sure I knew enough to identify my gift. If I had, I likely would have marred the authenticity of it and tried to fit it into a religious ordinance in my life. However, looking back now, seeing the way my life has gone, and how I have matured in my faith, I have a better idea of what my gift was. Work! Yes, work. Not many would look at work as a gift to be given to God. Isn't work the thing that interrupts our weekend leisure time? The very thing that I *must* do to help me buy all my toys? Yup, the very same. Work is my gift. It is the treasure of worship that I am able to lay at the feet of the very King of Kings.

When my parents separated, I was eight years old. I remember my Papa sitting me on his knee. He told me that, because of circumstances, he wouldn't be able to live with us anymore and that meant that I, being the oldest, would have to take on the role of 'man of the house.' It was a big burden for such a little guy, and I took it to heart. I wanted to be a provider for my family. That's what the 'man of the house' did. Remember how I talked about my mom, and her struggles to provide for us? Well, I needed to step up and help her and my siblings. So, what did I do? I got a job!

I began working for our local daily newspaper, *The Truro Daily News*, as a paperboy. Route 58. It was about three kilometers in length and had about thirty customers when I started. By the time I left it, two years later, it had grown to over one hundred customers. It was so large at that point, in fact, that they had to split it up into two separate routes to get anyone to take it on. How did a young boy who hardly had enough physical strength to carry the paper bag most days, grow a small business?

Most kids who grew up in the seventies were familiar with the PBS TV show, *Mr. Rogers*. The *Mr. Rogers* theme song (now that song is stuck in my head for the rest of the day) ends with, "won't you be my neighbour?" Another big hit in that same period was *Sesame Street*. They used to do a segment that had its own song too: "These are the people in your neighbourhood." I guess, in some way, I was influenced by these songs. I began to see the people in my neighbourhood as just that - people in my neighbourhood.

There was a nice, lonely old lady on Johnson Avenue, who just needed someone to talk to. Everyday, I would stop and smile and ask her how her day was going. I couldn't take long because I had more papers to deliver. For a few moments, though, she had contact with someone.

Then, there was the couple on Dunromin Avenue. Their children were all grown up with children of their own. They no longer lived nearby, and were caught up in their own lives. To this couple, I became a grandchild, as such. They would even spoil me too! Every week after collecting payment, I would be given a big chocolate bar.

I found that the more customers I had, the more lives I would become part of. I loved it. The money was nice too! I managed to buy my first bike with my tip money. A bike allowed me to go faster too, which in turn allowed me to get more customers.

A little guy with a strong work ethic was impacting a whole neighbourhood just by doing work. I didn't view it as ministry then, but that's what it was. I discovered that I had an ability to earn money and get to know people. I believe that job was one of the most satisfying and influential experiences of my childhood.

Work is the gift that I lay before the King of Kings daily. It isn't always easy. There are days that are tough for sure. But, for me, it is amazing that I can give back to him, with open hands, something that he has blessed me with. The Drummer Boy may have been little, but he gave all he had, and all that he was to the King, and the King smiled back at him.

My first real job came when I turned sixteen. I started working at one of the local grocery stores as a bag boy/stock filler. It was a fun place to work. One of the things we enjoyed the most was eating the damaged food. Often, when we were stocking shelves or unloading trucks, bags of food would get damaged. Nothing was wrong with the food, it just couldn't be sold. When it was damaged, a manager was meant to sign off on the damage and the food would go into the staff break rooms for us to share. This was a nice little reward for us. Unfortunately, like a lot of things in life, it was exploited by some of the guys. I would be down in the stock room and hear, "Oops, this bag of chips just happened to break as I was opening the box, I guess I'll have to eat it!" I knew full well that the bag didn't break accidentally, but one of the guys decided that he wanted something to eat when he went on his break. There was a lot of that kind of thing happening. I didn't like it, nor did I participate in it. I just kept my nose out of things and did my own work.

Another thing I didn't like to do was goof off at work. I believed that I was there to do a job and wanted to get the work done. In fact, I used to compete with myself everyday to do more. I liked the challenge of being better everyday than the day before.

These examples make me sound like a robot who felt he was better than everyone else. That wasn't the case at all. I respected my boss and the job that I had to do. I also knew that, as a Christian, people would be watching me. I guess, knowing that people were watching me in the workplace, motivated me to do the best job I could, without compromising.

Several years later, I was working for another company in a different community. I had to pop into the local grocery store to pick up a few supplies. As I was going in, I ran into a young fellow that I used to work with back then. He recognized me first. He then thanked me. I was confused as to why. He said that he remembered working with me and he remembered how I didn't get involved in the foolishness that most of the guys were doing. I just worked hard everyday. He said that it had inspired him to change his work ethic to try to keep up with me. He said he was now a manager for a grocery chain, and he believed that my example had helped him out. I was surprised to see the way God had used my gift of work to bless someone else.

God showed me that work is a gift he can use to impact people. No matter how big or how small you may feel your job is, do it for the glory of God, and who knows the lives *you* will be able to impact.

Chapter 2

LIKE A KID IN A CANDY STORE

Finding the Path of Ministry For You

*M*ost of us remember being a six-year old kid. Life was a little simpler then, now that we look back on things. Not a lot of life-altering decisions needed to be made. Well, not until you entered *the candy store!* If you were like me, your eyes would light up when you walked in. There was candy everywhere! Chewy candy. Hard candy. Colourful candy. Sour candy. The list went on. Being that six-year old kid, and having parents who cared for my future health, I was always told I could only pick one. Only one! What if I pick the Gummy Bears? Will the Sour Patch Kids start to cry? If I choose the Hubba Bubba, might the Love Hearts feel unloved? So many choices. What if I pick the wrong one? Will I regret it when I get home?

This felt like so much stress. At the end of the day, a difficult decision may feel huge and life-altering when, in fact, it is just like picking a piece of candy. There is no wrong choice. It is all a great treat!

Our oldest child, Ash is in Grade twelve and the big question that he, and most of his friends, are facing is: "What am I going to do with my life?" It's a big decision to make, for sure. We often think that this is the time to choose who and what you are going to be for the rest of your life. The truth is, most people will change jobs/careers many times in their life. If you had told me when I was in high school that I would be a restaurant owner at some point, I probably would have laughed out loud.

Nonetheless, this is a huge decision. Some are able to pick a path rather easily. They walk into the 'career store' and just know what they want - the perfect fit for their interests and talents. For others, it is a little more complex, just like that kid in the candy store. There are lots of colourful choices and various flavours. If I make a choice for *A*, will I miss out on *B* or *C*? If I choose *C*, will my parents be okay with it? What if I choose the wrong path?

Sometimes I think we make things more complicated than they need to be. There may not be a right or wrong choice.

When I was growing up, the common misconception was that to serve God, I mean, really serve God, the only options were to be a pastor or a missionary. The most noble sacrifices were to either go off to Bible College or to some foreign country.

In 1992, I joined the fray and went to Bible College. It was an interesting experience for me. I went because I felt God was calling me to minister to people. He had been developing different gifts and abilities in me that led me to believe that I would make a great pastor some day. When I talked to some of the other kids and asked why they were there, most had a similar response. We were all full of life and on fire for God. We were going to change the world one sermon at a time.

The more time I spent at the college, the more I began to realize that I was changing; we were all changing. We were starting to become like the Pharisees of old. I remember a group of us going to a youth group at one of the local churches, to help out. We thought we knew so much. The youth pastor was teaching and using an object lesson which we felt was a little too secular. When there was a short break in the activity, I remember him coming over to us and saying that if we weren't going to be a help or support, then we would be better off leaving. He knew his kids and the best way to get through to them. In retrospect, he was correct. We were so caught up with being right, that we failed to be real.

When I went home at Christmas after that semester, I began to question my calling. While I was trying to deal with the struggle of being right versus being real, my home church was going through a split. It is always a sad thing to see a once strong congregation self destruct with in-fighting. The whole thing showed me the ugly side of church politics. This convinced me that a career as a pastor was not for me. My personality was too fiery to show the grace and patience that is needed to deal with the politics. I didn't go back to Bible College.

When many heard of my decision, they felt that I had compromised and thrown away a gift that God had given me. I must admit, I almost felt the same way. I mean, being a pastor is one of the most noble, sacrificial callings that one could have. What was I going to do now? Had I really fallen away from God, like many thought? Was it possible to be a minister for God without actually being a minister for God? I guess I was going to find out!

Please don't interpret my experience as a slight against pastors or missionaries. I have a tremendous amount of respect for them. In fact, some of the most influential people in my life have been pastors. Pastor Bob was my youth pastor when I was a teen. He showed me what it was to love and know God in the midst of his own trials. Pastor Lindsay, one of my senior pastors, showed me what it was to show grace to others when grace was all he could give. I hold them with very high esteem, as they helped to mould and shape the man I am today.

This passage in Ephesians details the purpose of the work laid out by God for pastors and ministers:

> *"And he gave the apostles, the prophets, the evangelists, the shepherds and teachers, to equip the saints for the work of ministry, for building up the body of Christ, until we all attain to the unity of the faith and of the knowledge of the Son of God." Ephesians 4:11–13*

God has called some to be apostles, some evangelists, some shepherds, and some teachers. He gives these gifts to build us up, to teach us and guide us, to shepherd us and lead us. He equips us for the work of ministry; for the building up of the body of Christ. These occupations are part the foundation and support that we need as we are being built up. They help form the church that is his body. We are that church. Our purpose is to take that support and use it, with the help of God, to transform our world. We are built up so that we can go out. We need to go out into whatever occupation God has called us. It is possible to be a minister for God while working in that office. It is possible to be a minister for God while working in that garage. And, as I have found, it is possible to be a minister for God while working in that restaurant.

So, what should you choose as a career if you want to serve God? Well, I would ask: what are the desires or passions of your heart? This is often a clue as to what God is preparing you for.

Psalm 37:4 reminds us to delight ourselves in the Lord and he will give us the desires of our heart. Those desires are put there by him. Trust him. Commit your way to him. Let him be your guide. Wait patiently for him. Your desire might be towards pulling wrenches. It could be using a wooden spoon. It could be an obsession with math and numbers. Those desires are part of who you are, and could very well be the way God is leading you. Remember, to truly serve God, we must be authentic to *all* that God has created us to be. We must keep our mind and heart open to God and his leading.

Several years ago, I got the dreaded pink slip from my employer. It was only about a month before Christmas, so the timing was kind of rough. I remember being so much in shock, that even after my boss gave me the news, I continued to work for about another half hour. I busily entered data into my computer. It wasn't until she came back to my office, that I realized it was over. I had never been let go from a job before. This came as a surprise because it wasn't related to any performance issues on my part. It was just the way the economy was looking for the future.

It all happened shortly after 9/11. Most of our company sales were to the United States. With new regulations coming into play, shipping product over the border wasn't as simple as it had once been. My bosses felt there was no way, in the short term, that they could continue to employ me. After I left, I went to see Joanne at her job, to break the news to her. What a trooper she was. She helped me to hold my head high and offered encouragement that everything was going to be okay.

The next couple of months were difficult for us as we struggled to pay our bills. I needed to find a new job. I did a lot of searching for God and his direction during this time. There were several sales jobs available around the area but I didn't feel comfortable taking one. My heart wasn't in sales after the most recent setback. Where was I to go? I thought back to which job I had felt most comfortable with and most passionate about. It was my job in management with Tim Hortons. I had loved working with food. I had loved working with customers. God was directing me to a new career, based on the passion that he had created in me. A short time later, I accepted a Restaurant General Manager position with a national franchise. Based on the job qualifications, I really should not have gotten the job. But God is not limited by such things. He wanted me back in the food industry and he made a way for me.

God has called some to plant, some to water, and some to harvest. Some fill the role of pastors, teachers and shepherds. Some are asked to fill other roles. Regardless of where God has called you to be, that is your ministry. That is where you are to live Christ before the masses. We must be willing to listen to God and let him guide us, right where we are.

In addition to a desire to be used by God to reach others, our choice of vocation is very much a training ground for our development as well. I have learned so much about myself and about God, right in the middle of my workplace. Sometimes we are in a place for our benefit and sometimes it is for others. In every case, God has a purpose in it.

For example, the same sales job that had kept me on the road and away from my wife, had helped to bring me out of my shell to become comfortable talking to people. The job had involved quite a bit of cold calling. Not just cold calling on an average employee, but some of the top executives in the industry. I was scared stiff a lot of days. But God helped me to develop courage. He developed in me an ability to and strive to push through situations where I wasn't comfortable. I learned to take the risk. That workplace was a training ground for me in so many ways. God was equipping me to do his work.

God has a plan for me - for each one of us. It may feel as though the most important thing is nailing down the long-term plans of God for your life, but the reality is, he calls us to live in each and every moment. As I look back on my life - at the various places I have worked or studied - I realize that there were no mistakes. Each step I took, each job I worked, was preparing me to be in the 'now' of where God has me. Take the 'now' of where you are and use it to impact those who are in your sphere of influence.

It's easy to become overwhelmed as we try to discover God's plan for our lives. We can feel like a kid in a candy store. But God is not limited by our choices. He will use whatever path we choose to teach us to become a blessing to others in our workplace – whatever that workplace may be.

Chapter 3

I JUST WANT TO
BE A SHEEP

Seeing People as Children of God

"I just wanna be a sheep, baa, baa, baa, baa
I just wanna be a sheep, baa, baa, baa, baa
I pray the Lord my soul to keep
I just wanna be a sheep, baa, baa, baa, baa"

*I*t's a song that was written by Brian M Howard back the seventies. Many of us have been singing it in church since we were little. I guarantee that it will probably ring through your mind the rest of the day now. You are welcome! I often chuckled at the simplicity of it. Where's the challenge, lyrically? What doctrine is it trying to teach or reinforce? Well, this song, oddly enough, has been on my mind for a few weeks, as I work through what it means to view my workplace as my ministry.

In subsequent verses, it says, "I don't wanna be a hypocrite… they're not hip with it," and "I don't wanna be a Pharisee…they're not fair, you see." Hypocrite? Pharisee? Could these words be used to describe me? Well, yes! They have been, and unless I let God work in my life, they will continue to be.

Joanne and I opened our restaurant almost six years-ago. We felt strongly that this was to be our ministry for God. At the time, we were still working out what that really meant. In fact, we are still being shown, almost daily, what this means. One thing that began to stand out for us was the *Christian Bubble* in which we were living. We would sit in our pew at church on Sunday and feel quite comfortable. We had our friends and family around us, most of whom shared the same doctrine as us. We weren't really challenged to look outside our comfort zone. The sermons and the singing made us feel good about ourselves. Everything seemed right.

Then, Monday morning would come. We would get up and enter the *real world*. Our day began by bussing to work or walking the kids to school. Our time was spent with customers and co-workers. Sometimes we would stop at the grocery store or the mall on the way home. Our day was filled with so many interactions with people who weren't in our little *Christian Bubble*. The conversations we had and the images that we saw often didn't match what we had experienced in our pew on Sunday morning. We were, in fact, living in two separate worlds. For us, that was a problem. How could we be authentic with ourselves, with others, and with God, if our life was in constant conflict?

On Sundays, we felt like hypocrites, knowing we were striving to place ourselves inside that *Christian Bubble*. While the other days we felt like Pharisees, constantly judging the actions and motives of those around us. How does one find balance - the ability to function, in authenticity? The last verse of that little song says, "Just wanna be a child of God...walkin' the same path He trod." The only way this was going to work for us, was to find the balance of simply being a child of God, and viewing others as children of God too.

The first thing we needed to do was put aside the attitude of religious superiority we found in our hearts. How often do we, as Christians, judge people we come in contact with? We are quick to judge them. We see their choices and not the people behind the choices.

A good friend of mine named Paul, runs a small drop in centre in the downtown of my home city, Halifax. It is called Grace Street Level Mission. He works with the poor and marginalized on a daily basis. Paul has seen the need to balance the authenticity of being a child of God himself, with the necessity of seeing the people he serves as the same, whether they have discovered it for themselves yet, or not.

A couple of years ago, he took a few of us on what he called a *street walk*. This involved us walking around the downtown area of our city at night. We didn't just go on the well-lit, main sidewalks.

We walked down the back alleys. We saw a man sleeping in a dumpster behind a restaurant. We found a dark corner that was filled with empty liquor bottles and used drug paraphernalia. This walk opened our eyes. We were flabbergasted that all this was going on, right in the heart of our downtown.

Paul walked us through the typical life of a street-engaged person. Where do they sleep? What do they eat? What happens if they need to use the bathroom? If they are an addict, what must they do to get their next fix? It is quite scary to hear some of the self-deprecating things that people will do. They will do the obvious, by stealing things to sell. But they will also sell themselves. The shame that accompanies those on the street is beyond what we, in our little bubbles of middle income suburbia, can even imagine.

We walked by one older fellow pan-handling on the corner. Paul reached into his pocket, and pulled out a few bucks. He bent down and talked to him for a moment, and then gave him the money. The self-righteous Christian in me cringed at the thought of giving a *beggar* money. Doesn't Paul realize that he will likely just spend it on drugs? Yes, he does. After we walked on, he explained that, by giving him a little bit of money and stopping to talk to him as a fellow human being, he was giving him dignity in addition to money. Those few dollars may be spent on drugs, but they may also be spent on food. When we give, we often give with conditions. I will provide you with this, but you can't use it for that particular thing. When we do that, are we really giving freely? Paul gave him money, which may have saved him from degrading himself a bit that night. He also gave him something more. He saw him as a person, a child of God, and talked to him accordingly. I have seen people walk by, and look at people on the street with more contempt than any stray dog that might be begging for scraps. When did we stop looking at people as human?

It is important for us to examine our lives for sin. We need to keep short accounts with God, for our own transgressions. But God has not asked us to judge others. That is his job. It is the Holy Spirit who is responsible to convict of sin, not us. God has not called us to be bouncers at the door of Christianity. What he has called us to do, is to view people, first and foremost, as children of God. We are to love them, and show them compassion. We are to let our lives be lived before them in such a way that they see God.

There is a need, in this world, for authenticity. Kids these days crave it, and run from anything that feels fake or ingenuine. To make a difference in my workplace, I first had to find out who God was. I have been discovering that he is so much bigger than my little pharisaical life had made him out to be. When I discovered more of who he was, I was compelled to change how I interacted with people. Instead of being focused on changing who they were, I became more concerned with changing my view of them, through the eyes of God. Authentic interactions lead to authentic conversations. To allow God to minister through me, I must be authentic.

Going back to that last verse of the song, "Just wanna be a child of God…walkin' in the path he trod." Look at the path He trod. Beggar on the street? He talked to him. Tax collector? He ate with him. Leper? He touched him. In each and every case, he viewed them as children of God, and interacted with them as such. Can I really do anything less?

Look at this passage and see where you fit? I know who I want to identify with. I pray that God will continue to help me.

"He also told this parable to some who trusted in themselves that they were righteous, and treated others with contempt: "Two men went up into the temple to pray, one a Pharisee and

the other a tax collector. The Pharisee, standing by himself, prayed thus: 'God, I thank you that I am not like other men, extortioners, unjust, adulterers, or even like this tax collector. I fast twice a week; I give tithes of all that I get.' But the tax collector, standing far off, would not even lift up his eyes to heaven, but beat his breast, saying, 'God, be merciful to me, a sinner!' I tell you, this man went down to his house justified, rather than the other. For everyone who exalts himself will be humbled, but the one who humbles himself will be exalted." Luke 18:9–14

It is my prayer for my life, and yours, that we learn to be less concerned about being *right* and more concerned about being *real*. May God take us from being Pharisees and hypocrites, and use us to show his love to those in our workplaces. Let us walk the path that he trod!

Chapter 4

KEEP THAT LINE MOVING

Meeting People Where They Are

"Zacchaeus was a wee little man and a wee little man was he. He climbed into a sycamore tree for the Lord he wanted to see." Remember that little tune? I used to sing that with the kids in Sunday School. As I am writing today, it serves the purpose of reminding me about how God deals with each of us. This passage, in Luke 19, is the little story from which this song is based.

"He entered Jericho and was passing through. And behold, there was a man named Zacchaeus. He was a chief tax collector and was rich. And he was seeking to see who Jesus was, but on account of the crowd he could not, because he was small in stature. So, he ran on ahead and climbed up into a sycamore tree to see him, for he was about to pass that way. And when Jesus came to the place, he looked up and said to him, "Zacchaeus, hurry and come down, for I must stay at your house today." So, he hurried and came down and received him joyfully. And when they saw it, they all grumbled, "He has gone in to be the guest of a man who is a sinner." And Zacchaeus stood and said to the Lord, "Behold, Lord, the half of my goods I give to the poor. And if I have defrauded anyone of anything, I restore it fourfold." And Jesus said to him, "Today salvation has come to this house, since he also is a son of Abraham. For the Son of Man came to seek and to save the lost." Luke 19:1–10

A simple acknowledgement and validation as a person can accomplish so much. Jesus didn't go into this situation and say,

"Zacchaeus, you have sinned and wronged so many people. You need to repent and change your ways." No, he met him where he was and simply said, "You are important and valued; I am going to stay at your home." Salvation, both spiritual and social, came to his home that day.

A couple of years ago, I heard a message from one of our church leaders, Graeme. It started off as one of those ones where you elbow the person beside you, and you say, "I think this is for you." Funny thing - that day, I was sitting by myself. So, I guess I was meant to listen to this one. He talked about our purpose in ministry - in life. He talked about how we are to interact with others, reaching out to them for God. For years, I was taught that what we were to do, as Christians, was preach the Gospel. We are supposed to tell others of their sin and separation from God. Then, talk about the good grace of God in salvation. That was to be the focus of all our interactions. Witnessing for Christ. Preaching for Christ. Seeing sinners come to repentance. He alluded to these things in his message. Then he talked about something that I had never heard of before. He said that, although these things are good, it isn't our job to take on the outcome of our interactions with others. Let me explain. He said every life is the same in relation to our knowledge of God. You can think of each of our lives as individual timelines. We all start at zero. Zero represents no knowledge of God. It goes up to one hundred. Fifty represents our acceptance of Jesus on the cross for our sins. One hundred represents full knowledge of God. Each of us is somewhere on that line. The neat thing is, when you meet someone you have no idea of where they are on their timeline. They could be at forty-nine or they could be at twenty-five. Our purpose is to reach them where they are, and move them along the line. It shouldn't matter to us where they are. We simply need to show God to them, and see that they move forward and not

Swe   Hereafter
Ci   akery

REG   10 05 2018 20:30
                        000193

  1 Go slice 11 $8.00
  1 Go slice 11 $8.00
  1 Go slice 11 $8.00

    TAI $24.00
    TXI $3.60

    TL $27.60
    CREDIT $27.60

Thank you for coming in

backward, because of their interaction with us. Salvation is not our job, nor is it our sole purpose. This was an amazing thought for me. It is challenging and liberating at the same time. I have taken this ᵃˢ ᵐʸ ———— ᵉment in life: "Move them alor...

of sc ... udger of sin. He is a lover spiri ... r lives, both physical and him ... s, was to physically meet movi ... l come. Jesus engaged in

N ... ce for me to work this throu ... ere my staff are or where they a ... is to interact with them, and to ... gentle nudge, or it could be a b. ... nt each day. I just need to hav ... id see how he wants to direct i ... nister to my staff daily, leaving

It is ... ut when I do it usually change: ... how God chooses to speak t ... uake moments in life would b ... reach me. But instead, it's in th ... tly up behind me and whispers ... ice to teach you and help you ... oing just that in my workplac

Over ... evealing to me that I have been ... hinking. I have been so caught ... y ministry, that I've tended to ... someone else along the line. A ... ificant part of what I have bee ..., ᵃˢ ᵃ Christian and an employer. What

```
      SWEET HEREAFTER
        CHEESECAKERY
      6148 QUINPOOL RD
      HALIFAX        NS

          *********** 9467
CARD
CARD TYPE            INTERAC
ACCOUNT TYPE        CHEQUING
DATE              2018/10/05
TIME         0781 20:33:05
RECEIPT NUMBER
  C84075356-001-584-076-0
         --------------
PURCHASE
TOTAL
          $42.60
         --------------

Interac
A0000002771010
4971E45766125432
8080008000-6800
E17633EAA112663C
8080008000-7800

APPROVED
AUTH# 193305        00-001
THANK YOU

     CARDHOLDER COPY
```

God has been trying to teach me, however, is that I need to be moved along the line too. I need to grow. I need to learn. I need more of God.

For the most part, I have viewed my own *line-moving* as happening at church I have been moved by my brothers and sisters in Christ, with the music I listen to, almost any place but my workplace. I have spent a lot of time getting to know God while at work, but what I didn't understand was the impact the people in my workplace were to have on me. Joanne would often comment that God had brought certain people to help teach me patience or grace or some other quality that needed to be developed. I know I realized it at some level, but yesterday, after a challenging day with some of my staff, God showed me that he was choosing to use them to move me along the line.

It may be hard to believe, but I haven't always been the most patient and gracious person. In fact, patience has often been the last thing that I have been willing to exhibit. Yesterday just seemed like one of those days when everything goes wrong. The staff I was working with were making all kinds of mistakes. Nothing major, just little things that kept nagging at me, and taking my time and attention from the important things in my life, like lunch. They were dropping things that I would have to help clean up, asking me how to prepare things they have done many times. Again, it was all little things. I felt my blood pressure start to go up with each little thing. As I was approaching my breaking point, God said to me, "Are they doing these things on purpose?" "Well, no." "Then why are you so angry and frustrated? They can feel your frustration and, as a result, are being more tentative and consequently making more mistakes. Show them grace! Show them patience." It was tough for me to take that first step, but it was amazing to see how God changed my attitude, once I did. Operationally, things didn't change a whole lot, they were still struggling. But God had helped me to show them grace. At the end of the shift, one of them came to me and apologized for the trouble that she caused that day. Then she thanked me for being patient. It was just what she needed. Okay God, point taken. Today, she helped move me along the line.

Keeping the line moving sometimes also involves letting my staff move on to other employment. I strive to help them, not only become better employees, but better people too. What do you want to do with your life? What did you do yesterday to improve yourself? How are you going to change and challenge yourself today? Joanne often jokes that my kitchen helpers will move on after a year with me because they don't want to hear me rant anymore. She could be onto something there. It is truly wonderful to see a kid come through my door with, either no purpose, or so tired and damaged from previous stressful employment, that they can't see their way, then walk out some time later challenged and ready to take on the world.

One of the more touching moments I have experienced in this way, happened about two years ago. We had known Evelyn for a number of years. It all started when I used to take my kids shopping for groceries. Evelyn would often be working at one of the cash registers. She was not the fastest cashier but my kids absolutely loved her. She just wowed them every time we went through the cash, because she talked to them and really seemed to care about them. That is quite rare these days, as most cashiers are more concerned about pumping people through as quickly as they can. No matter how long her line up was, we had to go to her check out. So, we got to know her. Fast forward a few years, and Evelyn happened to come into my restaurant. I start talking to her and found out that she was now unemployed. Not only was she not working at that grocery store, but had since worked her way through several jobs with no success. After talking it over for a bit, we decided that she would be a good fit to work with us as a kitchen helper.

Each day, while we worked, we talked about what she wanted to do with her life, long term. It didn't take too long for her to go from having no idea, to deciding that she wanted a career as a baker. It was tough for her to find a program that she could get into, but she did it. After a year of working with me everyday, she took the plunge and went off to community college to become a baker.

About ten months later, I got a visit from Evelyn. She came in with a big grin on her face. She had done it, she had passed her course and was about to graduate. She also gave me the honour of being one of her guests at the graduation ceremony. It was probably one of the proudest moments I have ever had as an employer. To see where this young lady had started off when she walked through my doors, and now to see her walking across a stage receiving her diploma, was amazing. I was just talking to her last week, and she is absolutely loving her job as a cake baker for a local bakery. Moving them along the line is a very rewarding experience.

Sometimes it is quite difficult to encourage an employee when they want to move on. Operationally it can put a lot of stress on the business. If that person leaves, what are we going to do to fill those shifts? Emotionally, it stresses me right out. Personally, I have a bit of an aversion to change, especially if that change isn't initiated by me. I guess, when I look back at my life, a lot of that emotion stems from when my parents separated. When an employee decides to leave us, whether for good or bad, it can bring back those out-of-control feelings.

One young lady just gave us her notice yesterday. My initial reaction wasn't good. How am I going to fill those shifts on such short notice? She went on to say that she felt that it was a hard decision for her, but she knew that it would be the best thing for her, under the circumstances in her life. Although she is going to miss working with us, she knew that we would understand because we have always wanted the best for her. She appreciates the role that we have played in her life, to help make her a better person, and was quite thankful for it. Well, how can I argue with that? It has been wonderful having her as part of our team for these years, and now it is just time for us to help her move along the line.

Our lives here are filled with so many of these stories. I truly believe that just keeping things moving is one of the biggest parts of our ministry here. God has transformed us into a big functioning assembly line of sorts. He brings in the tired and weary through the front door, and we love them until they move along the line, right out the back door. Sometimes I feel that I am just here to enjoy the ride. God is good! I get to meet them where they are, show them the love and kindness of God, and let God do his wonderful work. I get to witness miracles every day.

Chapter 5

THY WILL BE DONE

Working Without Your Own Agenda

"Pray then like this:

Our Father in heaven, hallowed be your name.
Your kingdom come, your will be done, on
earth as it is in heaven."

Matthew 6:9–10

*H*ave you ever sat in a meeting without an agenda? How did it go? Chances are quite good that you didn't see as much accomplished as you would have liked. I love agendas. I love to have a clear picture of what is going to happen, and when. I don't like surprises or last-minute changes to an agenda that I have already set.

I remember a few years ago, when we were planning our first trip to Florida, for a Christmas vacation. I had a spreadsheet started with all our days planned out, along with the budget that we had set. For the most part, things went as planned, and that made me feel really good. Like I said, I like order and predictability.

When I decided to follow God's leading and open a restaurant with Joanne, I had no idea what to expect. I had a lot of industry experience, but nothing is ever truly predictable in the world of restaurants. I was scared. Over the years we have been open, I have been consistently tracking sales and other information with various spreadsheets. Joanne often jokes that I have spreadsheets to track my spreadsheets. These spreadsheets help me to project future sales. I can make decisions based on the numbers. These numbers help me decide things like: how much stock to order, how many cakes to bake, how many staff to hire, and how best to schedule them. This is all information that I feel comfortable working with. I can set a plan for how to run my business.

So, to recap, spreadsheets and agendas are my best friends. When God began to show me that my workplace was my ministry

I decided that it would be a good thing for me to try to plan it out. I would spend *X* amount of time doing *Y* activity and it would net *Z* results. It sounded like a perfect formula. My agenda included seeing any of my staff who weren't Christians come to know Christ as their Saviour. Not a bad agenda. The problem is, God doesn't work within our agendas. He does what he sees fit and not necessarily what we see fit.

> *"For my thoughts are not your thoughts, neither are your ways my ways, declares the Lord. For as the heavens are higher than the earth, so are my ways higher than your ways and my thoughts than your thoughts." Isaiah 55:8–9*

God will not always work in ways that we feel he should. There are times when he asks us to do things that aren't on our agenda. In fact, God has been teaching me to throw away my agenda. All that I had planned and purposed to do - throw it all away. That is really the only way that God is going to be able to do anything in my life and the lives of those around me. My purposes and plans need to be set aside and, moment by moment, I need to be asking what he would have me do.

Too often, I have tried to be God myself by influencing a situation and trying to force a conversation or an action in a way that God did not intend. I decide what God is doing in a person's life and try to bring it to fruition myself. I shouldn't do that but it is so tempting at times. What God has been teaching me, is to pray that little prayer at the beginning of this chapter. *"Our Father in Heaven, hallowed be Your name. Your kingdom come,* not my kingdom or my agenda, *on earth as it is in heaven."* Don't get me wrong, God does have a plan. He has a purpose for every single person. I believe that with all my heart. I also believe, just as strongly, that he has a part for me to play in that, in my workplace.

What he does not need is for me to try to figure it all out so I can do it myself. He has been teaching me to hold this work with open hands, ready to receive and, in turn, give to those who come into my sphere of influence. It is important to have open hands, because the moment I try to grab hold of something and make it something, it ceases to be something. Too often we try to make a ministry into a set of rules and guidelines that interfere with God's plans.

As an example, there is a young fellow I have been working with quite closely of late. Every morning we start the day together in the kitchen. We have had truly amazing conversations about everything from heavy metal music, to Celtic traditions, to politics and God. He is, no doubt, one of the most intriguing people that I have ever met. Almost every sentence starts with, "Did you know…" and, more often than not, I didn't. One of the best things I can do for him is just listen. Our theologies are quite different. I believe that for people to grow and learn they need a safe place to express ideas, without the fear of being rebuked. In my kitchen, we have that place. We each feel the freedom to share, without the other trying to argue and debate. I find it quite stimulating. Some things he has said have challenged me to think about what I believe and why. The old me would have looked at him, and said that he needed to be corrected. I would then have taken it upon myself to do it. The new me prays, "God reveal yourself to him. Reveal yourself to me. Help us to see you in this place and in these conversations." I need to say daily, "Not my will but yours be done, here on earth as it is in heaven."

This young fellow grew up being preached at all his life. The Christians would look at him, and do everything they could to change him. There was a lot of finger wagging and head shaking as they tried to shame him into changing. Fear tactics were used to exploit his emotions, in an attempt to facilitate him becoming a new creation. He doesn't need that. He just needs to be shown that there is a great, loving God. He doesn't need me to come in with some self-serving agenda. This morning, he paused part way through our conversation to thank me. He thanked me for not trying to change him by pushing religion on him. He thanked me for caring about him, and giving him a place where he felt valued. He thanked me for praying for him, while at the same time not pushing anything on him. I smiled at him. Inside, I almost wanted to cry. God was working in both of us because I left my agenda out of the picture.

In the previous chapter, we learned about moving people along the line. Trusting that God has a plan really is an extension of that. Look at where they are, and ask God to move them along. If he has a purpose for you in accomplishing that, then be ready. If he doesn't, be prepared to get out of the way and let him work. It is important for me to recognize that, although I refer to my workplace as my ministry, it is really God's ministry. I am quite fortunate to be along for the ride. When, viewed as God's ministry I can't help but humbly say, "Your will be done, God, your will be done!"

Chapter 6

LEAVE YOUR BURDENS
AT THE DOOR?

*God Will Use Your Trials to
Show Himself to Others*

I had a boss, years ago, who insisted that we are to live in the moment we are in. He would say, "You may have all kinds of things going on in your life, but when you are at work there's nothing you can do about those things. Focus on your work. Forget all the outside distractions. Get your job done." While I agree with him in principle, I don't think that it is entirely possible, nor should it be. Our burdens are part of who we are, our identity. While he is correct in saying that you may not be able to solve your problems while at work, I feel it isn't that simple. I do agree that it is very important to focus on work, during the work-day. As an employer, I most certainly would advocate for this - those customers can't serve themselves. However, there are times when our burdens follow us to work.

Leave your burdens at the door? At times, yes. However, as part of living Christ in the workplace, I think it is vital to live my burdens before others. This doesn't mean I should go around telling everyone within earshot my whole life story, with all its ups and downs. It means that I need to be ready to share my struggles, for my benefit, and for the benefit of others.

So often, we try to portray our lives as ones of perfection and strength. We get up and go to work everyday regardless of how we feel. Physical problems? Emotional stress? Spiritual burdens? None of that matters. We just put on the persona of Ken and Barbie. Perfect faces and perfect lives.

In this dog-eat-dog world, you can't show any kind of weakness. Weakness makes you stand out. Weakness makes you different. Weakness makes you the gossip of the workplace. No one likes to stand out for the wrong reasons, so we hide it. We put on our pre-packaged look and smile as we walk out the door.

Believe it or not, your co-workers don't have it all together like they may be letting on. That woman beside you has an abusive, alcoholic husband. The man in the next cubicle just found out that his wife has cancer. The young student who is coming in through the door is fighting depression, and doesn't know where to turn. The list goes on and on. Each carrying burdens that may feel very heavy. They are experiencing the loneliness of carrying their burdens on their own.

What about you? How are you doing? Put aside the persona and just pause, take a deep breath, and answer the question again. How are you really doing? Yeah, I know. You have a heavy load too!

I did the same thing. I have gone through that same deep breath exercise many times in my life. Some days I wasn't fine. Some weeks and months I wasn't fine. I remember quite clearly the day of Wednesday, November 26, 1997. I was at work in my office, when my administrative assistant told me that my wife was on the phone. She told me that my brother, who was living with my father in Sarnia, had called and wanted me to call him back. Well, I called him. In a moment, my life turned upside down.

My brother had come home to find my father laying on the couch, unresponsive. He had passed away peacefully from a heart attack several days earlier. I felt crushed as I hung up the phone. Every emotion I could think of was rushing through me, all at once. My Papa had passed away. After a few moments, I staggered out of my office with tears rolling down my cheeks. It was the first, and probably only, time I ever cried at work. When my administrative assistant asked me what had happened, I poured out my heart. She just listened. I told her that I had to leave right away to go home. She said that she would look after everything for me there, and to just go. She would contact my appointments and advise that I wouldn't be able to meet with them. She understood my pain. She cared for me and wanted to help me. That day, she helped minister to me through my obvious sorrow and pain.

The next weeks and months at work were difficult for me. Some days I would be able to laugh, and others I just wanted to curl up and not move a muscle. But, I continued on. I didn't hide my emotions or experiences. My co-workers were absolutely amazing. Living it out was a big help. I chose not to hide it or keep it all bottled-up inside. I was rewarded with tremendous support from my co-workers.

A few months later, the administrative assistant's father became ill. She had difficulty coping. It was my turn to help her. I listened and encouraged her through her worries. This is what real life is all about. When people stop putting on the Ken and Barbie faces and start embracing the raw emotions and challenges of every day life, we are all enriched.

Over the years, Joanne and I have had some big ups and downs. We saw the miscarriage of our first child, and then the joyous births of three others. We sold a house because of financial restraints and then later bought a new house, as God began to bless us with better finances. We dealt with Joanne's depression and many digestive issues. We dealt with me breaking different bones (I've broken so many I almost need a separate appendix at the end of this book.) We struggled through jobs that were a big stress on us. We lived through the excitement of opening our own business. So many amazing things have been a part of defining who we are. Each experience has been used by God to help us, and to help the many people who have worked with us and for us. The difficulties have made us more compassionate. They have helped us to give guidance to those who are going through similar circumstances. They have grown in us, courage to share with others enduring personal hardships. The purpose of these stories is not to draw attention to me but to show the depths that our lives can take us to. Living a raw, authentic life when you are walking beside people, impacts them in the most amazing way.

I read a book a number of years ago, by Ellen Gunderson Traylor, called *Samson*. In it, she makes a statement about Samson.

She says, "His strength was his weakness; in his blindness, he saw God." We don't like to show weakness because we are afraid. Well, Samson's strength, his self-sufficiency, was his weakness. When we refuse to admit that we are weak and choose to hold onto our own strength, we are, in fact, weak. Vulnerability should be our strength. When we are willing to let our guard down and be honest about our struggles, only then can we know true strength. Strength, and not weakness, is seen when we take off all the false pretences and live real.

It is our blindness, our state of being in weakness and vulnerability, that allows us to see God. Through weakness, we can see God at work in our lives, and in the lives of those around us. That man, who is facing cancer with courage and dignity, becomes a beacon of hope and courage for a co-worker dealing with her husband's cancer. When we insist on living our lives as spiritual hermits, in total isolation, we miss out on so much that God is doing. When we portray the image of strength, of rock solid, nothing-is-ever-wrong-in-my-life, we close our eyes to the majesty of what God is doing with our burdens.

I have been quite stressed and overwhelmed for the past few days. I'm not entirely sure why. I guess, in part, it would be business-related and, in part, it would be personal. Regardless of the reason, I have been sharing some of my stresses and concerns with my staff. They aren't necessarily big issues, but they show the staff, my co-workers, that I am a person too. It is days like these that I earn the right to say to them, "I get where you are in your life, because I have been there too!"

The confidence that people put in me, that vulnerability that they have shown in times of weakness, is such a beautiful and fragile thing. Joanne and I have walked with staff who have been abused. We have helped a young person who was addicted to drugs. We have listened to a mom who was overwhelmed with what to do with a problem child. We have comforted a teenager dealing with the hurt of losing her first love. It is a blessing for us to be in a place where we can be used by God to help minister to the weak and broken-hearted. But none of this would be possible if we weren't first willing to show that we, too, are vulnerable.

Leave your burdens at the door? No! Bring them right in with you, with all the messiness involved. Be willing to be used by God and, at the same time, let God use your co-workers to help you. Let the burdens of life be a blessing to all.

Chapter 7

OKAY GOD, LET'S TALK

God Hears and Speaks to the Heavy Heart

I have been told the average weight of an adult male's heart is ten ounces. Now, I don't have a scale in front of me to verify it, but today mine feels a lot heavier than that. Have you ever had a moment when your heart is heavy, and you have the need to express something, but can't verbalize it?

I came into work this morning and started to prepare for my day as usual - planning the day's bake and orders, replying to emails and social media messages, and reconciling the sales and paperwork from the day before. Nothing too out-of-the-ordinary. But there is a heaviness in my heart. I am not entirely sure what it is occupied with, but my thoughts are drawn to my staff. We discovered, in the last chapter, that many of them aren't okay. They are living through some rather large burdens. As an employer, my first reaction could be, "So what? As long as they do their jobs, it doesn't matter what is going on in their personal lives!" I can't do that. I am invested in them too much for that. I am compelled to help. But how? Well, I can provide them with a stable source of employment. I can give them a safe place, where they can be vulnerable and take refuge from life's challenges. I can be a listening ear. I can provide counsel. There is so much that I can and am doing.

Despite all this, I still feel a heaviness. In part, it feels physical but it goes so much deeper than that. It reaches my very soul. The only way I can describe it would be like when a friend has a close loved one pass away. You come to them and words just can't express how you feel. Those little platitudes of "Oh, he is in a better place," or "It's okay to feel sad," aren't enough. You know them all. What you really want to say can't be expressed in words.

I remember when my best friend's father passed away suddenly. He had been having some health issues for years, but nothing seemed imminent. When I found out that Richard had passed away, I dropped everything and went up home to see Rick.

His father had been like a father to me, as I was growing up. He had helped shape my life quite a bit. When I walked into Rick's parents' house and saw him, my heart sank. I didn't know what to say. My heart just ached for his loss. What could I say? I hugged him, then his mother. My heart was unable to express the grief. My heart was full of groaning that couldn't be uttered. Words escaped me. (That doesn't happen too often either!)

Today, at this moment, with this heaviness, I feel the desire to pray. But I don't know what to say. I asked God to show me a way to put into words what He placed on my heart, and this is the passage He showed me.

> *"Likewise, the Spirit helps us in our weakness. For we do not know what to pray for as we ought, but the Spirit himself intercedes for us with groanings too deep for words. And he who searches hearts knows what is the mind of the Spirit, because the Spirit intercedes for the saints according to the will of God. And we know that for those who love God all things work together for good, for those who are called according to his purpose." Romans 8:26–28*

The spirit hears the groaning of my heart. That is exactly what I needed to hear. All I can do is allow the Spirit to hear those groanings and answer them. That young man, God knows all about him and knows exactly what is needed, even if I don't. That young lady, God is doing something wonderful in her life even if I can't see it. God has shown me so much in my life that has convinced me that he is all-caring and all-capable of meeting these needs. All he asks me to do is pray. Prayer isn't to convince him to work or meet the needs. Prayer is for me - for me to be joined together with them in their struggles. It is a sign of solidarity, as such, between me and each one of my staff. The more I pray, the more I am compelled to care. The more I care, the more I am compelled to pray.

How can I be used by God as a vessel for his purpose if I haven't tuned my ears to hear what he has to say? Sometimes I feel that maybe I am stepping outside my purpose as an employer. I am concerned about things that are beyond my scope and responsibility. That may be true. But God has brought each of these people into my life for a reason. As I get to know them, with all their joys and sorrows, victories and defeats, excitement and grief, I find that I care more and more for them.

One of my favorite things is having one-on-one time with them. Just spending time talking. Talking and, in turn, listening, oddly enough, is the most effective way to get to know someone. I know, it was a shock to me when I discovered that! I always thought it was more effective to listen to rumours and jump to conclusions, but I guess I was wrong. To get to know someone, I must take time to communicate. There is a level of intimacy reached when I talk to someone. I find it quite intriguing to hear of the little things that make a person who they are. Listening allows me to see the true person before me. Talking and asking questions draws them out and helps me better understand them. The more I see them as more than just a payroll number, the more I care for them. They have some big burdens to carry. Often, they do it alone.

I remember growing up and being scolded for talking behind someone's back. Good boys just don't do that. It is not polite. Interestingly though, that is almost what prayer is like. I come to God and talk about my staff. I ask for wisdom and guidance in what I should say and do. I ask for God to work his great will and purpose in their lives. Those burdens that they are carrying, God can meet them in ways that I can't even imagine.

Each morning after I finish up my initial paperwork, I head up to the kitchen. I look at who I have scheduled to work that day, then I set about praying. I walk to each work station that they are going to occupy that day, and I pray for them out loud. I do it out loud because I feel that there is great power in that. I want Satan to hear and know that he is defeated - that he has no power here. I pray that God would put a hedge of protection around each work station, where Satan has no ability to work his deceit and lies.

God has been teaching me about the importance of praying for them, not just in generic terms, but with specifics. The challenges and triumphs that I have learned about them as I listened to them, now become my prayer list for them. I find it quite empowering to do this. There are times that I just don't have the words, and I rely on the Spirit to hear the groanings of my heart.

> *"Truly, truly, I say to you, whoever believes in me will also do the works that I do; and greater works than these will he do, because I am going to the Father. Whatever you ask in my name, this I will do, that the Father may be glorified in the Son. If you ask me anything in my name, I will do it." John 14:12–14*

"Come to me," he says. Come to Jesus with specific requests – he loves to hear and answer prayer.

When I started on this journey of prayer for my staff, I felt it was solely for their benefit. But I have found that this daily time in prayer also enriches my life. The more I talk to him, the more I know him, and feel known by him. My faith in him is increasing daily. I am convinced, more than ever, in the power that he possesses. I am also amazed at how he chooses to work. He does things in lives and situations that would never have even crossed my mind. God is truly amazing. There is power in prayer and I can't wait to get to work each morning and say, "Okay God, let's talk!"

Remember the Grinch who stole Christmas? What was his problem? His heart was three sizes too small! A small heart is the result of lack of care for others. My heart may be heavy, but that is a good thing. I am learning to embrace it. My heart draws me to God in prayer. It causes me to care for those in my workplace.

Chapter 8

PATIENCE IS A VIRTUE?

*Relax and be Willing to Help
Those Who Need Help*

"Therefore encourage one another and build one another up, just as you are doing. And we urge you, brothers, admonish the idle, encourage the fainthearted, help the weak, be patient with them all." 1 Thessalonians 5:11, 14–15

When I started working in this industry over twenty years ago, I had a full head of hair. It was full. It was thick. It looked amazing. Now I have very little left to show for it. I really believe that this is caused by my staff and co-workers over the years, because baldness doesn't run in my family. Little side note: I may not have much hair on my head but I do have a nice beard which I didn't have twenty plus years ago. If anyone asks if I am losing my hair, I say "Nope, it's just sliding down my face."

There are times at work when I get so frustrated I want to pull what's left of my hair out. On those days, I need to remind myself that my workplace is my ministry. It's not easy. One employee shows up late for the fifth time in a five-day work week. Another, inexplicably, has forgotten how to do a task that they have been doing almost every day. And another just keeps making a mess in the kitchen. It's enough to make my patience wear as thin as my hairline. Paul reminds us, though, to have patience with all. Patience that may not be natural to us, but that is given by the very God of patience. Need an example? Try turning fishermen into fishers of men without patience. Jesus shows us what it is to be the ultimate admonisher, encourager, and helper. He was living this out in *his* workplace; our world. If our purpose is to live Christ, our workplace provides an opportunity to do so every day.

I have often struggled to choose patience in stressful situations. Sometimes anger and frustration have been more readily displayed in my past than patience. I am thinking back, as I write this, to all the broken toes that I have had from kicking things in anger. The very hands I am using to type this paragraph have been injured because of a lack of patience. I am not proud of the way I have acted many times in my life.

One Sunday morning at home stands out in my mind as an example. My kids were quite young at the time - aged one, three, and five. Anyone who is a parent knows that, with kids that age, one of the hardest things to get is rest. A moment of peace. A moment of silence. A moment without 'let's cry and fight for sake of it and make so much noise that Papa can't get any sleep after a hard of week at work.'

Well, on this Sunday morning, unfortunately, I reached a tipping point. I got up and came out of my room and yelled at the kids, my wife, and the whole world. I just wanted to get a few more moments of sleep! I went back into my room where my anger boiled to the point that I just wanted to hit something. What could I hit? The soft pillow on my bed? Too soft. The mattress? Again, too soft. How about the wall? Perfect! Nice and hard. As a bonus, if I aim just right, I might be able to find the stud in the wall that I had been looking for to hang a mirror. Bingo! One broken hand and a nice mark on the wall indicating a stud later, I realized that I may have over-reacted a little bit.

I learned something that day. I learned that I have an anger issue. I learned that patience wasn't a virtue that I naturally displayed. I learned that it can be quite embarrassing to have to go to work later that day and explain how I broke my hand. I would like to say that I haven't had any further outbursts like this in my life, but I would be lying. However, God has taught me much over the years since. His patience with me and his gentle admonitions, have helped me to be a better husband, father, employer, and person. Patience may not be a natural virtue that

I possess, but God is developing it in me. I am thankful for the ways he is using my workplace to do that.

1Thessalonians 5:11 tells us to encourage one another and build each other up. For me, as an employer and as a Christian, this is non-negotiable. It must mark who I am. There are many times that I have needed encouragement in the workplace and I have gotten it through the actions or words of my staff. One young fellow that worked for me comes to mind. At times, things can get a little challenging when dealing with customers. The demands, the miscommunications, the unrealistic expectations, are all overwhelming. Sometimes, I just want to grumble and get frustrated. This young man, full of wisdom, would often remind me to be thankful. Yes, it may be difficult, and I may be completely justified in my frustration, but I need to be thankful for the customer who is willing to spend their money to provide my wages. Encourage one another. It is a beautiful thing to see. Sometimes I receive the encouragement, and sometimes I am called upon to give it.

Part of my purpose is to help each of my staff to be better, more complete, people. Ultimately, I would like to see them find God, but that may not be what God has called me to do. Each person has a story. Each person has something that they need to work through, as a person and an employee. Some are idle. Some are fainthearted. Some are weak. My workplace needs to be a safe place for them to work through some of these things.

Admonish the idle. What does it mean to admonish? It means to caution, advise, or counsel against something. It means to reprove or scold, especially in a mild and good-willed manner. It means to urge to a duty or remind of one's obligations.

Picture yourself back in high school (Whoa! I can't believe I wore that shirt with those pants.) Hands up if you liked to do homework. Okay, so maybe some of you liked to do it. Most of us would have rather done anything else. I know I did. Thankfully, I had Mr. Campbell who would gently admonish me and remind me that the passing grade I needed in his English class wouldn't be possible without doing homework. I had a simple duty as a student - to learn. It was not hard for me to be idle in this. The occasional admonishing was necessary to help me to become a more complete person, and to fulfill my obligations to myself and those around me. Incidentally, this book wouldn't be possible if he hadn't kept pushing me to continue to write assignment after assignment after assignment after…you get the picture.

What does all this have to do with the workplace? Well, remember that employee that was late for the fifth time in a five-day work week? He needs to be admonished today. I am not feeling the most patient. But patience is what he needs. I am not going to excuse his lateness, or pretend that it's okay for him to be late. I am going to use this as an opportunity to teach him about his obligation to himself and his workplace. I am going to help him work through the 'why' of his being late. I am going to help him find some solutions as to how to prevent it from happening again. I am going to help him understand the repercussions if it continues to happen. Will it happen again? It is quite possible, but God has called me to show patience with him. How many times has God been patient with me over the same things. I don't ever recall hearing him say, "That's it! I am done with this Colin fellow! He is as dense as a block of hardwood. Never again am I going to try and admonish him. I am finished!" Living Christ is to admonish and show patience.

Encourage the faint-hearted. To be faint-hearted is to be timid; cowardly; lacking courage. Life is full of big, scary experiences and, at times, can be very overwhelming. Some who are faced with difficulties in life, simply say, "Bring it on! Challenge? I eat those for breakfast. What? Is that the best you can throw at me?" Not everyone is like that. For some, just getting out of bed each day, is all they can handle. They may be feeling the fear of habitual failure. They have been so beaten up by life, and by those in their life, that they lack the courage to fight anymore. For some, they may feel paralyzed by the unknown. "I messed up yesterday and I don't know if I can face the consequences of that." Being late everyday may be a symptom of this very thing. In addition to admonishing, maybe we need to do a little encouraging as well. Some may be faint-hearted and lacking courage because they have no idea where the road in life is, let alone where it may be taking them. I need to help them. I need to encourage them.

There is one thing that I probably should clarify in all this. Unless you are in an occupation that directly involves some form of counselling, some of this may fall outside of your abilities and training. I am not suggesting that you take the place of professional help, that many people need. If that is needed, help them find the right professional. What I am suggesting is to work within the abilities that God has given you. God can equip you for the work that he has for you. Be prepared and be willing to do whatever part God has for you to play in their life experience.

Help the weak. About eight years-ago I hurt my back at work. It was a tough experience for me physically, mentally, and emotionally. I have never liked to admit I need help. My life has always been marked by the 'push through even if it hurts and get it done at all cost' mentality. So, for me to go down this way aggravated me. I don't like being weak. I don't like limitations. I have a job to do and I must see it through. "You know what, Colin? Life isn't like that. Sometimes you have weakness and you need help! We all have moments of weakness. Yours wasn't the physical limitations of your back. It was your ego!" What? Who just said that? It's true, we all experience weakness sometimes. What amazed me through that experience is how the job still got done. My lovely, and often wiser than me, wife, stepped up and helped with things, not only at work, but at home too. My staff worked extra hours or did tasks that they had never done before. I had an incredible team around me, who moved out of their comfort zones to help me when I was weak. I was weak and I needed help, and others provided that help. I truly feel that I am a stronger person now, as a result. My back still causes me grief from time to time, but my ego and warped sense of duty are coming around.

There will be times throughout our lives when we need help in the workplace. We may be weak and need a strong arm to help hold us up. I wear a back-brace from time to time, to help with the pressure on my back muscles. In the same way, I can be supportive to my co-workers and employees at the times when they are experiencing weakness.

Admonish the idle, encourage the faint-hearted, help the weak. All with patience. This is part of what it means to live Christ in the workplace.

Chapter 9

FOLLOW THE LEADER

Don't Tell Me Christ, Show Me Christ

Hide and Seek, Simon Says, and *Red Light/Green Light* are all games that we played quite a bit as kids. I loved them. All the kids in our apartment building would come outside on warm summer evenings to play games until our parents called us in for the night.

As much as I enjoyed those games, my favorite had to be *Follow the Leader,* especially if I was the leader. The leader had such power and control. As a young fellow who was considered vertically challenged, it was a great way to assert some level of authority. (Insert hand wringing and evil laugh of absolute power.) I could make people follow me wherever I wanted them to. And they had to hop on one foot while going backwards as much as I wanted. I learned very early though, that I had to be a little careful, because the next leader might like to assert some measure of revenge. The lesson I learned was this: be careful how you lead, because sometimes you may also have to follow.

I remember a line from a Spiderman movie. Uncle Ben says to Peter, "With great power comes great responsibility!" This is so true with leadership. You may have great power in your workplace, but you also have a great responsibility to those with whom you work. Look no further than Darth Vader. How did the whole absolute power thing work out for him?

Every workplace needs to be a team. Yes, there is a leader or leaders, but there also needs to be followers. If there are too many leaders and not enough followers, I guarantee it will be a dysfunctional workplace. Being a good follower is a wonderful gift. It is surely an important characteristic we need when Jesus tells us to take up our cross and follow him. We are not told to lead him. Being a follower who lives out the grace of God is like that light on a hill that draws people to him.

A fellow that I worked with at a grocery store when I was younger, really showed me the importance and value of being a follower in the workplace. His name is Don Timmons. As I write that name, I realize that I haven't thought of him in years. He was probably one of the gentlest men that I have ever worked with. Don't get me wrong, there were times when he would stand his ground with our co-workers or management, but he always did so with respect. As a young, part-time employee, I had the chance to work closely with him on stock nights. He took the time to mentor me, and I am quite thankful for that. When he was asked to do something, he did it. He had his list of stock to fill, and that was his focus. He wasn't worried about what anyone else had to do. He didn't concern himself with trying to make others do their work. He just did his own thing. His work was always done quickly and efficiently and, more often than not, it included a smile. He just loved being a follower. I asked him one day about why he always seemed so happy and seemed to love doing his work. I found out that he was a Christian, and he felt it was important to work for his boss as though he was working for Christ himself. He didn't feel the need to do anything but a good job. He had a genuine contentment with just being a good worker. What a testimony for Christ. There is tremendous kingdom value in being a good follower.

Most of my working career has been spent in some form of leadership or management. I realized, early in my career, that to be a good leader, I had to learn to be a good follower. I have always believed that people follow leaders who inspire them and treat them with respect. One important rule I believe in, for example, is to never ask anyone to do anything I'm not prepared to do myself. Sometimes it surprises those I work with. They say, "You are the manager, you don't have to do that job." Cleaning the grease trap is one of the grossest jobs in a restaurant. All the stuff that goes down the drain builds up into a big bin of smelly sludge. I can't tell you how many times I have surprised new staff when they see me up to my elbows in that sludge, scooping it out into a bucket.

I think back to my days at KFC for another example. We had, at one time, a promotion that ran on Tuesdays called *Toonie Tuesday*. Two dollars would get you two pieces of chicken and a small fries. It was the craziest day of the week. Most staff would either work the lunch rush or the supper rush. I always felt it was important for me to work both. It was exhausting, but the respect I gained from my staff, as a result, was noticeable. If they see that I am willing to work in the trenches with them, they are more prone to follow me where I need to lead them.

There was a young fellow who worked for me at one point, who very much wanted to be promoted to an assistant manager position. Everyday he would ask me if I was going to promote him. It was a great goal, but it was the motivation behind it that caused me concern. He looked at the management position as being the boss. He wanted to have the ability and authority to boss people around. He only valued leadership for the authority that came with it. He failed to see the importance of leading people, and not just directing people. You can direct, and they may do what has been laid out, but if you lead them and encourage them to follow you, it will make so much difference. Incidentally, I never promoted him, and he left a few months later in frustration. It made me sad that he took that action. He had some great qualities that could have made him a good leader, but the thought of power was too intoxicating for him. Leadership should never be about power.

Jesus was the ultimate leader but he didn't treat his 'position' as one of authority to be lorded over his followers. He led by example, but he also sought to include his followers in all that he did. He was preparing them and setting them up to be successful in their ministry.

"Now the eleven disciples went to Galilee, to the mountain to which Jesus had directed

them. And when they saw him they worshiped him, but some doubted. And Jesus came and said to them, "All authority in heaven and on earth has been given to me. Go therefore and make disciples of all nations, baptizing them in the name of the Father and of the Son and of the Holy Spirit, teaching them to observe all that I have commanded you. And behold, I am with you always, to the end of the age."
Matthew 28:16–20

Jesus had just spent the last number of years teaching his disciples. He used parables and other teachings to instruct them. Nothing was as profound, though, as his life. He became obedient to his Father to the point that he was willing to be led to the cross. Everything he did while he was here demonstrated the love of God. He was a leader, leading by example and showing what it meant to be a follower. When he was leaving, he sent a comforter to continue to lead us in his absence.

Jesus has inspired me. I live this out in my workplace as I attempt to lead as Jesus did. I want to inspire my staff and set them up for success - not only as employees, but as people. I have found that the dictator style of management is often concerned about profits above people. I believe that if I focus on the people, the profits will follow. Money and profitability is important but the reward for leading people is so much greater. I hope to let my leadership bring glory to God. This is one time when I think it is important to follow *The Leader*.

I was reflecting upon this chapter, this morning, with my father-in-law, Bob. He told me about two different bosses that he has had during his working career, and the differences in the ways they led.

One supervisor would stroll into the shop where he worked, and just start barking orders and directing the guys around. It didn't matter what they were in the middle of doing, they were required to just stop, drop everything, and do what they were told.

The other supervisor worked beside him everyday. He never *told* Bob what to do, but *asked* him to do things that needed attention. It is now forty years later, and Bob still has tremendous respect for this supervisor.

One man directs and the other one leads. Who would you rather work for? Who would you rather be looked upon as? I know what my choice would be.

If I am going to be like Jesus, I need to know how to lead with gentleness and care. I need to be a good follower too. Jesus gave us the perfect example of how to lead with authority without abusing power.

Chapter 10

GO STAND IN THE CORNER

Sometimes it is Good to be the Bad Cop

I remember the first time I said a *bad word*. I was about six years old. My mother dragged me right into the bathroom and washed my mouth out with soap. To this day, I am not entirely sure why parents in the seventies felt that was an effective way to curb potty-mouth, but they did it.

A few years later, I remember my poor, overwhelmed mother chasing my younger brother and I through the kitchen. With wooden spoon in hand, she was looking to instill some semblance of punishment in our fighting ways. Boy, we really used to frustrate her. When she did catch me, I would stick out my hip for her to hit instead of my bottom. The spoon would break every time. I am sure that if I had been a dog, my mother would have dropped me off at the nearest pound.

Discipline and punishment were common occurrences in my life. Most of the time, it was deserved. I remember being very concerned about my mother's well-being. I was always confused about why she would choose to punish me. Each time, she would say, "This is going to hurt me more than it hurts you!" I knew how much it was going to hurt me, so I would plead for her pain. "Don't do it mom, it is just going to hurt you!"

"Whoever spares the rod hates his son, but he who loves him is diligent to discipline him."

Proverbs 13:24

Each stage of my life had discipline that was age specific. It may have been time-out, standing in the corner, or taking away the telephone. That one always hurt. How's a young man suppose to impress the ladies if he can't talk on the phone? The most effective one was probably standing in the corner. It was so effective that my wife uses it on me to this day. Standing in the corner drove me nuts because there was nothing that I could do. I just had to stand there and think about how I was going to get back at my brother for tattling on me.

I have been making light of my mother and her discipline of me when I was younger. It really wasn't that bad. I was a pretty good kid, overall. I am thankful for the discipline that she did administer. It was a sign that she cared for me, and that she had my best interest in mind. Discipline is necessary for the normal development of any child. How can I function as an adult in an adult world, if I have never learned discipline? Thanks Mom!

My role as a boss isn't that much different than that of a parent. Just like a parent needs to make tough decisions at times, holding their children accountable, I need to do the same as a boss. Sometimes I need to provide praise and encouragement, while other times I need to administer corrective action and discipline. It is a package deal and requires a delicate balance that must be treated with respect. I can either build up and improve my staff, or I can tear them down and damage them, if I am not able to achieve that balance. Just like a parent, I need to make sure that I never administer corrective action in anger. It is not meant to be punishment, but a prompt to create positive change in behaviour.

One of the things that sets us all up for success, is to set clear expectations. I set the tone for a lot of those things right in the interview process. I tell potential employees what I expect from them, and how they can expect me to support them. If they aren't willing to follow that, then we don't move forward. Once they are hired, we train them. Again, the purpose is to set them up for success. The more they understand, the more likely it will be that they will follow the processes and rules.

There will be times, no matter how clear I have been, or how thorough the training was, that they will make errors in judgment and need to have a short chat in my office. I will say that this is not my favorite part of the job. I don't wake up in the morning and say, "Boy I hope that one of my staff does something wrong so that we can sit in my office and deal with it!" It may not be my favorite part, but it is a very important part. If I choose to ignore wrong behaviour, big or small, I am doing them a disservice. Just like a parent, they need me to hold them accountable. Incidentally, I don't recall ever having to fire an employee. We would talk it out and come to a mutual understanding that this no longer the appropriate place for them to work. Well, if you take away the semantics, I probably did. It just sounds so much better this way.

As I am writing this, my thoughts go back to a time when I had to discipline a lady that was working for me. Emotionally, it was one of the toughest things I've had to do as a manager. Operationally, I knew what I had to do and just made the choice to do it.

Tammy was a good employee. Dependable, hard working, and pleasant with customers and co-workers. What happened was something that had never even crossed my mind with her. Tammy was a grandmother of three. Her son had been running into some financial difficulties and was forced to move back into the house with Tammy and her husband. Tammy's husband was off work on disability, so the whole family was forced to survive on her income, which was only slightly better than minimum wage. It was not a lot of money to feed so many mouths.

I began to realize that something was wrong when my inventory levels were off consistently on a few different products. I was very good at tracking items and knowing what was going on with my inventory. So, when things weren't balancing, I began to do some further investigating.

One Monday morning, I came in to see that more product was missing. I went to the camera system and saw that Tammy had put a bag of the frozen product into her backpack and took it home. My heart just sank. I knew why she was taking the food, but I couldn't turn a blind eye. It needed to be dealt with. I notified my area manager and told her what I was going to do. I set up a time for Tammy to come into the store before it opened the next day, when no other staff were around. I am a big believer that correction or discipline should always be done in private. One of the worst things you can do as a boss is call someone out in front of her peers. Before she came in, I was feeling sick to my stomach. Again, emotionally I was not wanting to do this, but I knew it had to be done. When I confronted her, she initially denied taking anything. Once I showed her the evidence, she admitted her guilt. The progressive discipline policy of the company dictated that she was to be suspended for one week. She chose to resign her position instead. It was a sad ending to her career.

Discipline is not a fun process. One thing I learned from Tammy's story was the importance of separating emotion from facts. Emotionally, you can totally feel for the person. I mean, they are real people with real lives, but you aren't doing them or your workplace any favours by not dealing with discipline issues. The workplace needs order to function properly. Discipline should always be fair, predictable, and consistent. There should be no surprises. Discipline should also be done with grace. It is easy to lose sight of the fact that this is an actual person sitting across from your desk. One thing that Jesus was amazing at doing, was humbling without humiliating. When a disciple needed to be corrected or rebuked, Jesus showed grace and compassion. He didn't say, "That's okay. I know you feel bad and didn't mean to do that. Let's just forget about it." No, he dealt with things in a fair, consistent manner and the disciples were better for it. I pray that God will continue to help me do what is right, and not what is easy when it comes to dealing with my staff. I care for each one of them, and will do all that I can to make sure that I deal with them fairly.

One final example of discipline comes from another young lady that worked for me. This young lady had a habitual issue with timeliness. If she had four shifts in a week, she was late for three of them. Not a great deal of lateness, just five to six minutes, but it was happening consistently. We had several talks about the importance of being at work on time, and it just didn't seem to make much difference. I could have ignored the lateness, but it was something that she needed to learn to overcome. I wouldn't be helping her by letting the issue continue unchecked.

Finally, I set the consequences. Every time she was late, I would schedule her one less shift on the next schedule. By setting the consequences clearly, it allowed me to take the emotion out of the situation, when it happened again. If she was late, I wasn't going to be angry. I wasn't going to make her feel bad. At the end of the day, it was her choice, so she needed to face it, not me. A week after we had our talk, she was late. She then lost a shift on the next schedule. It happened a few more times over the next month or two, but it was improving. She was beginning to understand the need to be on time, and how it affected the workplace when she wasn't. Things haven't been perfect since then, but I have seen a tremendous improvement in her. My job wasn't to punish for the sake of punishing. My job was to help this young lady to grow and improve herself. It is my hope that this will help her to be a better person and employee in the future. I wonder if making her stand in the corner would have helped!

At the end of the day, discipline is not fun, but it is very necessary. I need to remember to be clear and to be fair. I should use it to correct negative behaviour, not as punishment. Using Christ as my example helps me to administer discipline with grace and compassion. I hope that as my staff move on through their lives, they will be able to look back and appreciate the hard things that I have done as much as I appreciate what my mother did to prepare me for adulthood.

Chapter 11

GRANOLA BARS
AND DORITOS

Kindness Shows the Love of God

I remember being in Sunday School when I was ten years old. We had the best class. No girls allowed. This was an all guys class. Being a ten-year old boy, that was the best thing that I could think of. Well, I thought it was the best until I met my teacher, Jim Atkinson. We all thought Jim had the best job ever. He worked in a chocolate factory. Who wouldn't want to do that? All chocolate, all the time. We could only image how amazing it would be. One of the things that stands out about my years in that class is the chocolates he would bring for us. They were used as treats, rewards, whatever he could think of. (I wonder if he saw the value of his workplace as his ministry.) He probably had one of the most consistent attendance sheets in the entire Sunday School program. I know, at that age, I wasn't the most interested in God or learning all those Bible verses. Jim, through those chocolates, did something that I look back on now with extreme gratefulness. He may have tricked me into memorizing the books of the Bible, but I learned them. He may have used the chocolates to motivate me to read the Bible and listen to lessons, but it worked. I learned some great foundational truths because of his class.

When I look back, it isn't the chocolates themselves that stand out. They were just a vehicle for Jim to show his interest and kindness toward us. What I realize now is that he truly did care for me. Being without a father, I often felt left out and under-developed, socially. I mean, all my friends had their dads around to teach them some of the basic things of life. I didn't have that.

I remember many Saturdays when Jim would pop by and pick me up. He was in the process of clearing a lot so he could build a house. We spent a number of afternoons cutting trees and moving the brush and logs around. I'm sure I probably didn't contribute a great deal. In fact, I possibly slowed him down. But the kindness that he showed me has stuck with me these thirty-three years later.

I am quite thankful, not only for Jim, but for all the 'Jims' that have entered my life. I'm thankful for all the little things done out of kindness that have impacted me for a lifetime.

A few weeks ago, I saw generosity in action with my staff. We had a new girl start work with us. She had just moved to the city and was sharing an apartment with her boyfriend and a few other friends. When she moved here she didn't have a lot with her. In fact, she had not much more than her clothes and a few books. Jennifer discovered that she was sleeping on the floor in her apartment because she had no bed. Well, that just wouldn't do for Jennifer. She called her mother and asked about the spare mattress they had at home. Her mother gave the blessing to pass it on, and Jennifer offered it to her. She was so excited to be given such a gift. It was a beautiful display of kindness offered freely.

There is so much power in generosity. Especially generosity that is not expected. We have a contract with a fellow who picks up our garbage everyday. When we hired him a number of years ago, we settled on a particular price. After a couple of years, I felt God telling me to pay him more. In this day and age, when most business owners are trying to cut corners and save money wherever they can, God was asking me to give more. So, I went to him and told him that I valued the work that he was doing, and felt I should be paying him more. He was in shock at first. But the smile that came over his face was priceless. I realized that I was not only giving him more money, but I was showing him respect and appreciation too.

It may sound crazy, but I have found that the more I show kindness, the more kindness I want to show. It is fun to look at my daily life at work to see if there are ways, big or small, where I can show people how valuable they are to me. You never know what impact an act of kindness or generosity will have on a life.

Every Monday, Tuesday, and Thursday, Timothy comes in to work for his 8:00 am shift. Mornings and Timothy don't always get along. I tell you though, I am quite impressed by him, he has never been late. Now, I have found that, although he is always present and on time physically, mentally he is often still home in bed. He needs a little boost to get him going, so I always have a pot of hot coffee brewed for him. It may not seem like much, but to him, it says, "I get where you are and I want to help you." Ahhh caffeine - the great motivator.

How I choose to compensate my employees is very important. I believe that it must not only be fair, but it should go above and beyond. Joanne and I decided that, for us to put our money where are mouth was, we would pay more than minimum wage. By paying more, we show our staff we value them. We recognize their importance, and the fact that we couldn't do this job without them. It isn't just about generosity for the sake of generosity. It is a demonstration of the value we place on them.

We also feel it is important to pay them all the same. Whether they are a new employee, or one that has been with us for a couple of years, both receive the same pay. This reflects the value of potential – and the fact that our employees are more than the things they can do for us. No matter who they are, they are important. From time to time, we increase the wage that we pay, and when we do, we increase it for all. While we appreciate hard work and tenure, the wage we pay isn't tied to those things. It shows that everyone is on equal ground with us.

Over the years, many of our staff have come to refer to Joanne as their work mom. She is always cooking for them, or making them some kind of treat. One of their favorite snacks is nachos. Most evenings it can get hectic, and at times, they need to be able to stop and take a deep breath. Also, they expend a lot of energy when they are in hustle-mode all night. Joanne will pull out the nachos, shred some cheese, get some sour cream and salsa ready, and they will munch away. Again, this is just a little thing, but it speaks to the value that she places on them.

A by-product of those nacho moments, is the conversations that she has with them. She has been known to talk relationships, theology, and education with them, often in the same conversation. She meets them where they are, and talks about whatever is relevant to them. If you ask some of them, the nachos are great, but these little moments of conversation are what stick with them. It's an example of how real, life-changing conversations are enhanced by a little gesture of giving.

Another simple thing she has done is set up a staff appreciation box in the staff room. This little box is filled with gifts of food: granola bars, Doritos, apple sauce, candy - whatever Joanne can find at the grocery store. The staff will arrive early for their shift and fuel up on snacks. They may grab some for their pockets as they are getting ready to walk home. Doesn't everyone like a little treat? Joanne knows that, often, these students are coming to work directly from school. It's a lot easier to begin a busy evening shift with a little food in the belly. And nothing says *love*, to a student, like food!

It is the little things that can make a difference. Showing we care doesn't have to cost a lot, but it can definitely accomplish a lot. How can we *tell* them we care, if we aren't willing to *show* them we care? Using the power of generosity to minister to people in our workplace is a joy, and more powerful than we thought!

I like to challenge myself to be like my Sunday School teacher, Jim, looking for little ways I can show kindness that may impact a person for a lifetime. Didn't Jesus do the same? Consider the feeding of the five thousand with two little fishes and five loaves of bread. I don't think the people were on the brink of starvation that day. But, Jesus wanted to show them kindness, appreciation, and compassion. How many were impacted beyond the five thousand? How many can be impacted in our lives in the same way? If you have the chance, give with all generosity and kindness.

Chapter 12

THESE EYES ARE WATCHING YOU

Live Like You Belong to Christ

(*T*)ake a walk down the street and look in the store windows. Walk through a mall or into a bank - there are cameras everywhere. Take a few moments and check out social media - video uploads and selfies are everywhere too. Everyone has a camera. Everyone is looking for things that will catch attention. Years ago, there was the fear that *Big Brother* was watching everything we did. I am not a conspiracy theorist, but this is becoming more and more of a reality. The truth is people are always watching us.

Everywhere I go, I am being observed by someone. I go to the mall, and I hear people excitedly shouting, "Hey it's the cheesecake guy!" I drop in to get a bite to eat at my favorite fish and chips place, and I hear, "Hey it's Colin from Sweet Hereafter!" Now don't get me wrong, I don't have throngs of fans following my every move. There are no paparazzi camped outside my home. But I have come to realize that people are aware of who I am, a lot of the time. Okay, so big deal; a few people know who I am. Well, if people are watching me, I need to be aware that they are taking note of all that I do. If I walk into a restaurant and treat my server with contempt, it is going to reflect on my business. If I cause a scene at the local department store, guess who that reflects on? Yup, me. Note of full disclosure here: I did that a few weeks-ago when trying to buy a winter jacket that was advertised on sale. For the record, tiny fine print exclusions on sale items, that a man of my age has a hard time reading, are not cool. I did it all. Voice raised, check! Demand to see the manager, check! Grumble loudly when leaving, check! Guilt about how I treated that poor part-time employee, check! Go back after, with my tail tucked, to apologize for how I treated him, check! Whether anyone knew who I was, was totally irrelevant at that moment. I needed to make things right for my benefit, but more importantly for his. No one needs to be treated with disrespect.

I had another incident this weekend. Boy, am I ever a work in progress! Our local internet provider decided, in all its wisdom, on a Friday afternoon, to disconnect my business email address, making it unusable. Not a good thing for a business, for sure. I called Friday night to ask for some help, and got nowhere. The guy was pleasant, and although I wasn't the most amicable, we did get through the conversation. Unfortunately, the solution was not something he was able to provide at that time, and I was instructed to call back in the morning. Well, I did that too! Several conversations with a few different departments were getting me nowhere. It would all have to wait for Monday morning, when the business department would re-open. I was quite close to totally losing it. I was about to express my complete dissatisfaction with the whole situation, when I remembered that I was calling about my business. Did I want to have that kind of behavior reflect upon me or my business? It's not the best way for a proper business man to act, let alone a follower of Christ. So, I politely thanked the young lady for all her help, and hung up the phone. Although, I didn't punch anything, I did let my anger ruin the rest of my day. I was a total bear. Conversations with my staff were nothing more than grunts and quick responses. Poor Joanne got nothing but a cold stare when she was getting ready to go home. Who am I supposed to be representing again? So much for showing the love of Christ that day.

Everything we do, reflects on who we represent. One restaurant I worked for had a rule that we were never to wear our uniform in any competitor's restaurant. They made sure we understood that, whenever we wore our uniform, we were representing the company. Whether we were on the time-clock or not, didn't matter. We were accountable for our actions. I saw a guy get let go because of some questionable behaviour in the local community, while wearing his uniform. Someone is always watching. As Christians, we don't necessarily wear uniforms, but we do represent Someone.

One thing that I try to instill in my staff is the importance of being honorable in our dealings with customers. We sell cheesecake. Just cheesecake. When you only sell one product, you'd better do it well. One of our mottos is, "If in doubt, throw it out!" Meaning, if there is any chance that product is not up to the standard it should be, do not serve it. Some customers may not be aware or even care, but we know. We may get a few dollars by selling the imperfect product, but we run the risk of losing that customer for life. We have an integrity standard that must be maintained. It is also important for my staff to see me consistently make that choice. They too, are watching me. If I am cheating the customer, then what is that saying about who I am and what I stand for.

I remember the first car I bought. I was nineteen years old. It was an '85, '86 and '87 Toyota Tercel. In essence, it was a Franken-car. It had parts from all three years. I bought it for $1500 from a Christian friend of mine. I had no clue what I was looking at when I bought it. What I knew about cars was that you put the key in the ignition and made sure that it had gas. I heard his sales pitch and trusted him because he was a Christian brother. Well, a few weeks after I bought it, the back strut broke. I spent a few hundred dollars fixing it. A short time later, the frame split behind both front wheels. That was a fun thing to have happen while going down the highway at 100 kilometers per hour with a car load of kids. Another buddy of mine welded it for me. The final straw came when the transmission went on me. I sold it for $200, less than six months after I bought it. I had gone back to my Christian friend to talk to him about the car, only to find that he had skipped town. I had naïvely trusted him because he was a Christian, and I totally got burned by doing so. I found out later that he had known full-well some of the problems that the car would have, but since he needed the money, he did what he had to do. I was not only broke as a result, but I was crushed that he had taken advantage of me. Looking back, that moment reinforced in me the importance of treating people properly in all business transactions. There is never an excuse to exploit or take advantage of someone.

As an employer, it should go without saying, that I need to treat my staff honestly. I had a previous employer who always rounded down the time clock punches for the employees. It troubled me that he was so willing to do this. He justified it by saying that he didn't want his labour costs to get out of control. He was so concerned about the pennies that he ended up losing dollars. Eventually, the staff found out what he was doing and complained. When it didn't change, many of them took it upon themselves to take back some value, by eating food without paying for it, or giving discounts to friends and family. Many also, as a sign of protest, would show up just as their shifts were to begin and would leave precisely as their shift ended, regardless of how busy things were. They were not going to give a single minute to him that he didn't deserve. The turnover rate in staff was also quite high, because they didn't feel valued by the employer. All in all, the way I treat people will be reflected back in how they treat me in return.

How we treat people - staff, friends - is very important. Sometimes they see it directly, other times it can be seen in our attitude toward them. Again, we are not just representing us, we are representing God. I know that I need to remind myself of this everyday. Today, Oh Lord, help me to live like I belong to you.

Chapter 13

WHAT, TAKE A DAY OFF?

Rest is Good For the Soul

*M*y name is Colin and I am a workaholic!

How do you tell a person whose gift is work that he needs to stop working? It may be just as easy to tell a bird not to fly, or a fish not to swim.

I am also hard-pressed to let go and let others do the work. I like to be in control. I like to know exactly what is going on. I need to know the numbers. I need to know that the work is being completed to my standards. It has been hard for me to learn to trust those around me. I train them, and then I must have faith in them to do things the way I want them done.

When I work, my workplace is neat and tidy. Everything is in its place. I am so particular, that I drew a line around my mixer on the steel table with a permanent marker, to make sure that no one moves it. My spatula is always in the same place. The egg shells are lined up in order so as to be counted at attention at any moment. I like order. Order represents efficiency. Efficiency represents the proper use of time. Time is the all-consuming focus of my personality.

When 'Hurricane Marla' would bake, I had to leave the kitchen. When she started to work, I wasn't sure what was going into the cake and what was going on the floor. When I would leave the room, day after day, an amazing thing would occur. The work would be done without me. It was a crazy revelation for me. Someone could step into my size eight shoes and fill them. Her cakes were wonderful. The orders were being filled. The kitchen was clean at the end. The world didn't collapse on itself. I found that I had time to *breathe*! What did I do with this new-found freedom? Well, I found more work to do, of course…that's just what I do.

I have always had a tendency to push myself. It's how I grow. It's how I develop and get stronger. I like competition. I get a thrill from 'talking trash' and trying to be better than someone else.

More than that, though, I like to be better than myself. Each day, I want to accomplish more than I did the day before. I want to, not only get more done, but I want to do it more efficiently. Life is always a competition. This can be a great thing. It has helped me to succeed at most things I do. But it can also be a negative thing when left unchecked.

When I was manager of a pizza restaurant, I loved working Fridays the best. We would put out about 300 pizzas on an average Friday. It took a lot of hard work and hustle to make it happen. My most productive role was what we called *landing*. This is where you take the pizzas out of the conveyor oven, cut them, and put them into boxes. On a typical Friday, we would have up to three people working the station, over a supper period. This station required extra effort to keep up with the pizzas being spit out of three ovens. I used to try motivating the younger guys by saying that they couldn't keep up with an old guy like me.

One Friday, I decided I was going to show the young guys what I was capable of doing. I say it was for the young guys, but it was probably a little more for my own ego. I drank an energy drink before the rush began. When you take someone who has a high metabolism, throw in a good dose of adrenalin, and then add in a large quantity of caffeine, you are just asking for trouble. I worked that station by myself for over an hour. It was hilarious, the guys were just getting in my way and slowing me down.

When I got home after that shift, I sat down on my sofa. I looked down at my chest because I was having a hard time breathing. I could see my heart pumping. I thought for sure I was going to have a heart attack. It had been fun, but I may have pushed myself to my limit that day. Pushing myself can be good. Pushing myself almost to the point of self-destruction, is not. That was the last time I tried to prove I was better than all the younger guys like that.

Incidentally, it was also the last time I had an energy drink. What I took from all this, is the realization that I have limits, and I need to respect those limits. Ignoring the physical signs that I am nearing the end of my rope is not something to be taken lightly. This can be a hard thing to accept. I am getting older, and I can't expect that I will be able to do the same things that I did when I was in my twenties. I am learning that that is okay. My limits may be changing, and that is something I need to accept, even as a workaholic.

My wife, Joanne, and I always joke about our different outlooks on life. She is a journey person. I am a destination kind of guy. I remember a Sunday afternoon a few years ago. We got out of church shortly after noon, and realized that we had no plans for the rest of the day. Nothing was demanding our attention. There were no schedules that needed to be kept. We were free! We decided that it would be a great opportunity to go down to the lovely Annapolis Valley for the day. Wolfville was our destination.

Target set! Go! That's what I was thinking. I didn't care how we would get there, just that we would get there. Joanne had a different view of how it would go. Wolfville was our *eventual* destination. The journey, in her mind, would take us down the back roads to visit every little yard sale and farmer's market she could find. If there was a quaint little shop along the way, she wanted to stop at it. One wanting to get there, and one wanting to be on the road to getting there, maybe. There seemed to be a difference of opinion as to what we should do. Well, there was for a short time anyway. Any man who is married would agree with me that, in this case, it should be all about the journey. So, journey is what we did.

To my surprise, I actually really enjoyed the journey. When I stopped focusing on timelines and kilometers, and relaxed, I could appreciate what Joanne saw in the journey. I also discovered some wonderful baked goods, some delicious beef jerky, and some extra calories. She didn't tell me that going slow could taste so good. Sometimes life can be about the journey.

A year or so ago, we did a series of sermons in our church fall initiative. One of the messages was called *The Spirit of Slow*. I felt God speaking to me about the importance of slowing down. We had just moved to the outskirts of the city a few months earlier. Before that, we had been living right in the middle of the hustle and bustle of the city suburbs. Sirens, traffic, and construction were the sounds of daily life. Out in our new home, it was different. When I went out to my vehicle in the morning, I was greeted by a chorus of small birds. The only traffic I saw were the squirrels running across my lawn. Construction? We had that too. A pair of chickadees were building a nest. The sermon about *slow* taught me that it is okay to have some down time. It taught me that I don't need to be busy working all the time.

It began to make perfect sense to me. So, what did I do? I planned some downtime. I bought a model kit to build. I dug out my guitar to continue teaching myself how to play. I came up with a number of planned, purposeful activities to occupy my new spirit of slow. Joanne graciously told me one day, "I think you are missing the point. If you are planning the activities like that, you are just replacing one form of work with another." She, as always, was correct.

I had grasped the concept mentally but was struggling to translate it into my life. I was still being bound by my obsession with time. Downtime still felt like a waste of time. The danger for me in not having the proper amount of downtime lies in the fact that I am going to burn out. When I crawl out of bed in the morning, my body reminds me that I am not that twenty-year old kid anymore. Muscles are tighter, reflexes are slower, memory is starting to fade. I joked this year, on my birthday, that I was finally starting to feel my age, but that I didn't think that twenty-nine would feel this old. My cousin pointed out that even twenty-nine will eventually feel old, when it happens every year.

Work is important, but so is rest. Rest not only allows my body to recover and rebuild itself, but it allows my mind to reboot and refresh as well. God has been showing me the importance of rest, not only for mind and body, but also for spirit. It is in the moments of quiet that I am able to hear God. It is in those times of reflection, that I am able to see all that he has been doing. I am able to express gratitude to him in a way that I can't do if I am going full-out, working all the time. He has been teaching me that, sometimes, it is important to just *be*. I don't need to have a purpose. I don't need to wear the hats of employer, teacher, parent or anything else. I just need to pause and exist in quiet. "Be still and know that I am God."

I am slowly starting to embrace this attitude of appreciating *slow*. My life is not always about the destination, but can also be about the journey. I am learning that early Sunday morning quiet time is part of the journey that God is bringing me on. Those moments when I just sit outside in the hammock and listen to the birds, are a necessary part of my growth. It's part of the journey. The slow walk down to the lake is not a waste of time but an embracing of time.

Jesus got this too. Many times, he would leave all that was going on around him to just go up to the mountains to pray. If the Son of God needs some quiet time away from work, how much more do I need it. Sometimes taking time away from work is the best thing I can do. I am coming to the realization that I need to control work, and not have work control me. Life, at times, is about the destination, for sure. But if you get there and you are exhausted and have lost the relationships you care about along the way, maybe you've missed the point of getting there. I am thankful for a wife and a God who understand the journey, and have encouraged me to embrace a spirit of slow.

Chapter 14

HOW'S YOUR BALANCE?

Your Family is Just as Important as Your Job

In April 1999, I added another title to my resume - father. The job description would include the obvious: late night feedings (well it would involve me waking up my wife to remind her that it was time to breast feed), diaper changing, and many long drives around the block to help get this little one to sleep. It would also include other things that I am not sure I was prepared for. I was now to be a provider, protector, and guide. It is a tremendous responsibility and it still weighs heavily on me. I am still, to this day, in awe of the responsibility that parents carry in raising children.

Like most things in my life, I took my role as a father quite seriously. The idea of being responsible for another life scared me – it still does, in fact. It was a task I had to commit to, wholeheartedly. It is a great journey that requires a significant commitment of my time and attention. At that time, my paid, full-time job was a sales position that kept me on the road a lot. When Joanne and I entered into, not only our marriage, but also into parenthood, we agreed that it would be a partnership. Couple this with the feelings of abandonment that came from growing up without my father around, and I decided that I couldn't continue with that job. I worried my job kept me away from home too much.

After my parents' divorce, when I was only eight, I experienced what it was like to have an absentee father. I made a vow to myself that, if God ever blessed me with the opportunity to be a father, I would be the best father I could be, and that would mean being present for my child or children. My sales job wouldn't work for that. I felt that it would be a compromise to stay with the company. My income wasn't the greatest at that point, but after two years of hard work, the commissions were just starting to come in. The residual income for the next few years would have taken a lot of pressure off our young family, for sure. However, I still needed to make this change. So I left and took another sales job that would keep me local. I went into my office in town every morning and was home every night for supper.

The most important thing I feel I can give my kids is to be present. Physically present, yes, but also emotionally present. I want them to know that they are important and that they should be treated accordingly. I want them to understand the importance of accountability to themselves and to others. Joanne and I have done all that we can, not only to love them, but also to show them what love looks like. They need to know how they deserve to be treated in life. To show them these things, I need to be there as a parent. That is my job.

Being there in the early days meant picking them up when they fell, wiping the blood off their knee, and putting on a cool Barbie Princess Band-Aid. These days, the issues are a little more complex. Tea parties and tiaras from the early days, have become walks around the neighbourhood, playing catch on the front lawn, and digging up holes for dead rabbits (Long story, but my son, Ash, has an interest in bones and dead things.)

We have had the opportunity to demonstrate love to our children in very tangible ways. Last Valentine's Day, we decided that our daughter Marcella was more important to us than money. You see, our lovely Marcella was the Valentine's gift that God gave Joanne and I on February 14, 2001. Owning a restaurant, especially a dessert restaurant, means that Valentine's Day is a very busy and lucrative day for us. We usually bring in about 20% of our monthly business on that one day.

Last year, Valentine's Day fell on a Sunday. As a small business, we have always been closed on Sundays. It is our personal conviction that we need one day a week where we can demonstrate to ourselves that God and family are a priority for us. So, on the Sunday in question, we were put to the test. Open for the day and reap the financial rewards, and avoid the backlash from customers, or stay closed and celebrate our daughter's birthday as a family. We chose Marcella.

It was a wonderful day. It reinforced to me, as much as to her and the rest of our family, that time together really is important. Our business didn't collapse as a result, and interestingly enough, we only had one social media comment about not being open. We also went on to have a strong month of sales, and ended up exceeding our planned budget for the month. I don't believe in a direct cause and effect system with God, but I do believe, wholeheartedly, that God honours those who honour him.

My workplace is my ministry, true, but my ministry also includes my home. My home is a significant part of the ministry I have before God. I believe that he has honoured and blessed our home in many ways, as we have sought to keep this key ministry before him.

When I am home, I try my best to *be* home. Paperwork and schedules still must be done, but so do other important things like helping the kids with their homework, going for a little walk together to check the mail, and teaching my daughter how to throw a baseball. I am learning quickly that I only have a short time with them before they are all grown up and off on their own. As a parent, I need to take what time I have to help prepare them for the life ahead.

As we continue this journey, and as our kids get older, we have been blessed to have them work for us. Not only do they get to learn about how to be a great employee, but they get to see God in action as well. Also, they can afford to pay for their own cell phones. Win/Win!

It has been a joy to have them work beside us. It has afforded us all the opportunity to get to know each other, outside of the family roles. Joanne and I aren't parents at work, but employers;

and they aren't our children, but employees. You get to know a much different side of each other when you take away the family roles and filters.

Ash, our oldest, works out front as a server. It absolutely blows my mind to see him work with customers. I watched him go from being a timid kid - nervous to even bring a drink over to a table - to one that jumps at the opportunity to handle the largest reservations by himself. He has a showmanship that reminds me a lot of me. He is also developing a drive to prove himself to himself. Just like me.

Marcella, our middle child, has recently taken on a back-of-house role, helping decorate cakes. During her shifts, it is often just the two of us with maybe a third helper around. These times have afforded me the opportunity to see a creative side of her I had never noticed before. She is learning to push herself and enjoy it. We have also discovered that she is able to get up at 7:00 am, even on the weekends.

Laurie, our youngest, has one of the best roles. Every September, the street our business is on has a little street festival. There are games and booths set up all along the street. Many of the restaurants, including ours, offer food samples. We put out about 1500 little cheesecake bites on that day. Laurie is my runner. I stand out front and chat with the public while handing out the bites. She is my go-between, taking empty trays back to the kitchen and bringing out full ones. It's hard work, but she looks forward to that day all year. I used to think that she was doing it just to be around me, but she informed me this year, jokingly, "It's all about the money!"

Bringing our children into our workplace has allowed us to facilitate the balanced life that is so important. We get to spend time together, but we also get to know each other in a deeper way. It helps our kids understand some of the pressures we face.

Often, they would see me come home from a hard day without any understanding or context for why I may be a little tired or cranky. Seeing what I do on a daily basis helps them to understand my exhaustion in the evenings.

I am a workaholic at times, but as I get older and wiser, I have been discovering that God requires me to be balanced. I need to be sure not to neglect the blessed opportunity I have been given to be a parent. My home is just as important a ministry as my restaurant. I pray God will continue to help me to be faithful in both.

Chapter 15

GOOD BYE DEAR FRIEND

Relationships Define Who God is

A few years ago, when I was working for a restaurant franchise, my boss decided to transfer me to Halifax. Operationally, it made sense. By this point, I was not only a Restaurant General Manager but also an Area Trainer. This meant that I was responsible for all new product training, new manager and supervisor training, as well as operational compliance audits. With most of our stores being in the Metro area, a transfer was inevitable. Halifax is an hour away from the town where we lived at the time, but we made the move. Life in the big city was something quite different from the small town where I had grown up. More traffic, more crime, and more complex commutes, all made life a little more interesting. When my move was complete, my boss decided that Wyse Road was the best location for me, as my home-base store. Wyse Road was known, informally, to us managers as *The Career Killer*. This store was in one of the roughest parts of the city, with one of the highest crime rates, and lowest average incomes. Many great managers had tried to conquer the challenges that this store provided, only to either quit or request a transfer out. Transferring out often led to being pushed back on the promotion list.

When my boss told me that this was where I was to be posted, I took it as a challenge. Those other managers had failed, but they weren't me. I could surely make this store thrive!?! My tenure there lasted seven months and ended with me resigning to take a job with another franchise. Those seven months were quite eventful. I had to deal with everything from a store that was literally collapsing around me because the building itself was so old, to flattened tires on my van, to armed robberies, to staff not showing up because they were in jail for various probation violations.

In some ways, I felt defeated. I had faced the challenge and had failed to succeed. Despite all the things I felt hadn't gone well, I did have one success I have been able to enjoy to this day: friendship.

Ronnie was a cook. He had been with the company for about twenty-five years. He had been moved from store to store, depending on what was most convenient for management at the time. Although, he had been with the company for all those years, he didn't feel valued or appreciated. Ronnie was a good, hard worker. He was loyal and always willing to do what was asked of him. Ronnie's problem, however, was that he couldn't read or write. As a result, many managers had treated him as a lesser employee. By the time I came along, Ronnie was feeling quite defeated and was looking to give up on his job. I took it upon myself to befriend him. I helped him with all his tests and certifications, reading him questions and recording answers for him. I made sure he got better shifts and wasn't just given the left overs that no one else wanted. As time went on, Ronnie became more than just an employee under my direction, he became a friend.

It was a hard day when I told Ronnie that I was moving on from that franchise. I had learned a lot about restaurant operations during my time there, but I think the legacy I cherish most is my friendship with Ronnie. It has been over ten years since I left, and I am still in contact with him. Every few weeks, he will pop by my store, or we will text or call each other. He still has some struggles and I continue to help him as best I can. My friendship with him reminds me that my ministry in the workplace has a legacy that transcends the workplace itself.

About a month ago, a dear employee came to me to tell me that she needed to give her notice and move on. Carolyn had been an employee of mine for over eight years - working not only in my current restaurant, Sweet Hereafter, but also at one of the previous places I managed. I knew something was on her mind that day because she was even more quiet than usual. When she asked if I had time to talk, I saw the tears in her eyes and knew she was getting the courage to tell me she was leaving. It was hard for both of us. Carolyn, her husband, and children have become like family over the years.

She wasn't leaving because she didn't like her job or because she wasn't being treated properly. It was just time for her to move on to another challenge in her life. Carolyn had moved to Canada from the Philippines, along with her family, to provide new education opportunities for her children. In the Philippines, she was a trained dentist. However, because of Canadian regulations, she was not able to practice here. For a number of years, she had been working on getting her certification in the State of California. She managed to do it. It made me very proud to see her work so hard to accomplish her goal. Now she is off to California to start a new phase of her life. It saddens me greatly to see her go, but I know it is best for her and her family.

As a parting gift, she commissioned a watercolor painting of our restaurant, that she gave to Joanne and I. It is actually the image you see on the front cover of this book. She also wrote a short note to us. I would like to share a little of it with you. She writes, "I want to thank you for always being there for me the past eight years. Thanks for the lessons learned and for the love and care you've always shown. One thing is for sure, our goodbye today will be just physical, for both of you will always be here in my heart, and will always be an integral part of my life. Thank you for your help and advice on my encounters with life's difficulties." The note goes on but I don't feel comfortable sharing any more.

God has shown me that friendship isn't just a bi-product of ministry but is essential for ministry. It is a reflection of the fact that I am being changed as much as those I hope to impact. I have been touched and overwhelmed by many people over the years that I can now call friends, as a result of working together. My legacy isn't seen in the financial results brought to the workplaces I have been part of. It is seen in the lives of those God has impacted through me.

Really, this is what it is all about. Impacting people for God in our workplace, happens when we are willing to live openly and honestly before others. When we treat our co-workers and employees with kindness and generosity, sharing our life with all its messiness and authenticity, we are showing them what it is to live Christ. Instead of saying how much we care, we must show them that we really do care. It is important to show them that we are real people, and not just concerned with appearing to be right. Workplace ministry is taking the time to get to know them, and praying for them, and asking God to use us as a vessel for his purpose in their lives. We can learn to be a true friend by being willing to lay aside our own agenda, and seeking God's guidance and help. The best way to build a ministry at work is to allow ourselves to be touched by the lives of those around us, and to see Jesus in them.

Joanne and I have chosen to offer up our workplace as a ministry. For us to do this we must recognize that people are more important than profits. Friendships are the evidence of that. They are our legacy.

As I come to the end of this book, I have become very much aware that this is not the end of the story. I have written but fifteen chapters of the story. It is my hope that you and I will use this as a starting point for God to work on. There is much more for us to learn about ministering in our workplaces.

Learn Christ, live Christ, work for Christ. Commit to being real versus being right. Use the Scriptures, the example of Jesus and the leading of the Holy Spirit, to help and encourage you as you start on your own journey of discovery in your workplace. It is a blessed thing to be used by God. Hold your hands open before him and let him work through you in your ministry.

CPSIA information can be obtained
at www.ICGtesting.com
Printed in the USA
LVOW11s0335260517
535885LV00001B/1/P